SEARCH THE SCRIPTURES

A THREE YEAR BIBLE STUDY COURSE

GENERAL EDITORS

THE REV. G. T. MANLEY
THE REV. H. W. OLDHAM

FIRST YEAR

THE INTER-VARSITY FELLOWSHIP
39 BEDFORD SQUARE, LONDON, W.C.1

Search the Scriptures (Revised), First Year

First Edition *1947*
Second Edition *1951*
Third Edition (revised order of study) . . *1955*
Fourth Edition *1960*

Made and printed in England by
STAPLES PRINTERS LIMITED
at their Rochester, Kent, establishment

PREFACE

THIS course of Bible reading was first issued in 1934 in response to a widespread demand from Christian students and others for a systematic plan which could be used daily in the Quiet Time. Its aim is to guide the reader through the whole Bible in three years, and it first appeared in six parts, each of which provided six months' study. The late Archdeacon H. E. Guillebaud compiled two of these booklets, Dr. B. F. C. Atkinson, the Rev. R. J. Cobb, Dr. F. D. Coggan, and the Rev. A. M. Stibbs, one each, and the Rev. G. T. Manley acted as General Editor.

This new and revised edition is the work of the late Rev. H. W. Oldham, assisted by a small band of helpers. Experience showed that the value of the course to students of the Bible would be increased if more explanatory notes were introduced, especially in those sections dealing with the more difficult biblical books. This has now been done with the two-fold aim of simplifying the course generally and of directing attention more closely to the actual text of Scripture.

The course now appears in three separately bound volumes (instead of six as previously) of which this is the first. Each provides one year's study. The plan of study, which is simplicity itself, is set out in the General Directions, which should be carefully read. In this new (third) edition some changes have been made in the order in which the books are studied during the first two years with the object of introducing more New Testament material during the early months. The original compilers and those who have assisted in preparing this revised edition are in close touch with the needs of students and know well the difficulty of sustained Bible study, and how many a hindrance Satan will put in the way. But they pray that the guidance here given, by the grace of God, may stimulate such a taste for His Word as to make the time daily spent upon it a delight as well as a source of strength.

G. T. MANLEY

PREFACE

CONTENTS

CONTENTS

GENERAL DIRECTIONS FOR STUDY

THE AIM OF THE COURSE

THIS is quite definite—to provide for university students and others a working scheme which will cover the text of the whole Bible in three years. There are many schemes which provide more extensive commentaries and notes, but the purpose here is to stimulate the personal study of those who will give to it at least twenty minutes daily.

A major question which arises at once is the relationship between intellectual study of the Bible and the Quiet Time.

'Your object in the Quiet Time is not so much to gather information as inspiration, and so you should discover what is the application of what you read to your then present circumstances and need. Turn the truth into terms of life, and use the Word to light and feed the fire of devotion.'*

As far as the present course is concerned, while the intellectual need certainly has not been disregarded, the compilers have endeavoured especially to provide for those who will desire to use the course *as part of their Quiet Time*, and to this end daily questions have been designed to bear as far as possible on the spiritual meaning and application of the passages. The great need is to gain a real knowledge of the text of the Bible itself, and this is where the whole emphasis is being placed day by day. Yet foremost for our practical lives must be the thought of the need of the Bible for *spiritual life and power*.

The following suggestions, originally put forward by Dr. Griffith Thomas, are offered for this devotional study:

* Dr. Graham Scroggie in *The Inter-Varsity Magazine*, Michaelmas Term, 1933.

1. Open all such occasions with prayer for the Holy Spirit's light (Ps. cxix. 18). This is most important. The knowledge of what the Bible says, or even a correct understanding of its meaning, will not of itself bring spiritual life and power. 'What is needed,' says Andrew Murray, 'is very simple: the determined refusal to attempt to deal with the written Word without the quickening Spirit. First, in a quiet act of worship, look to God to give and renew the workings of the Spirit within you; then, in a quiet act of faith, yield yourself to the power that dwells in you, and wait on Him, that not the mind alone, but the life in you, may be opened to receive the Word.'

2. Ask to be guided to some definite thought for *yourself*.

3. Dwell prayerfully on this thought thus given—Is it a counsel, a precept, a warning, a promise, an experience, a command?

4. When its meaning is clear, use it as the basis of a prayer for grace to realize it in experience.

5. Yield the whole soul in full surrender to its truth and power.

6. Link it on to truths already known, and thereby strengthen the chain of experience.

7. Trust God to reproduce it in your life that day.

THE NATURE OF THE COURSE

Keeping the above aims in view, the three sections of the Course each provide a year's study, in which the ground covered is grouped in weeks so that the Course may be started at any time, irrespective of date. The time is divided more or less equally between the New Testament and Psalms and the rest of the Old Testament. The assumption is made that not less than twenty minutes will be spent on the portion and questions daily, but, of course, the amount of text covered varies from day to day. When reading the Old Testament the portions are, roughly speaking, twice the length of those in the New Testament books.

THE USE OF THE COURSE

(a) *Requirements.*

While the Course can be used with the Authorized Version only, the following additional equipment will help the student to obtain the best results:

(i) *Authorized Version* and *Revised Version*. The Course is, in general, based upon the Authorized Version of the Bible, and can be profitably used with this alone; but to obtain the best results it is necessary also to have a Revised Version for consultation, preferably one with references. Indication is given in the daily questions and notes where the rendering of the Revised Version is of importance in the study of the portion.

There are also a number of modern translations, such as those by Moffatt, Weymouth, Way (Paul's Epistles only), and the excellent American Revised Standard Version of the New Testament published in 1946, to which occasional reference is made in the Course. It is not necessary for the user of the Course to possess these, but if he already has any of them, or has access to them, they will often throw light upon the meaning of a difficult passage.

(ii) *Two Note Books*, one an exercise book for rough notes and references, the other a loose-leaf or other good note book for more permanent records.

(iii) *A good concordance.*

(iv) *The New Bible Commentary*, a one-volume commentary on the whole Bible published by the Inter-Varsity Fellowship and designed primarily to enable the student to understand the meaning of the text.

(v) *The New Bible Handbook*, also published by the Inter-Varsity Fellowship, which takes into account the latest results of biblical and archaeological research. While no special time has been allowed in the Course for external reading of this kind, the Handbook will be found invaluable as a book of reference, and any additional time given to it will be amply rewarded. It contains a series of chapters dealing with general biblical subjects, and with the historical background of the Bible story; and provides also a much fuller introduction to the Bible books than is given in the present Course.

(b) *The Material Supplied in the Course.*

(i) *Introduction* and *Analysis* at the beginning of each book, to give some grasp of the contents at the outset. These should be read before beginning the study of the book and may be referred to again with advantage from time to time.

(ii) *The daily portions,* accompanied by questions, notes and references. The notes have been kept down to a minimum, and the attention of the student should be given to the questions, rather than to the notes.

(c) *The Actual Procedure.*

This must be settled individually, but an indication of two ways in which the material has been used may be valuable as a suggestion.

(i) Read the portion through, and jot down in the book for rough notes the main subject or subjects with which it deals. When a clear grasp of the general contents of the passage has been obtained, then write out answers to the questions, leaving a brief time at the end for practical application.

(ii) Look at the questions first and deal with them during the first reading of the passage, jotting down rough notes on them. Perhaps there will be time for a second reading.

Whatever the actual procedure may be, it is essential to realize that answering questions is simply a means to an end. Hence, at some stage, time should be given to such prayerful meditation as will lead to a personal appropriation of the spiritual message, and if desired, the recording of spiritual impressions.

There will be days when a section proves too much for the

allotted time. In such cases a choice between the questions should be made, and one of the questions be left over. It is inadvisable to carry the question over into the next day, so as to fall out of step with the progress of the Course. A better plan is to devote some extra time on Sundays, both for going back to questions that have not been dealt with, and also for writing up the rough notes made n the daily study into a permanent record.

(d) *Comparing Results.*

A final note may be added regarding sharing results with others. While our own individual work in seeking to get to know the Word of God for ourselves is the most important thing, and worth any number of analyses or points which we obtain second hand, nevertheless there are great advantages also in comparing notes with others working on the same basis at the same time. By this is not meant organized Group study, which is another method of studying the Bible, and for which specially prepared outlines are issued by the Inter-Varsity Fellowship. What we are speaking of now is informal exchange of thought with one or more friends on points arising out of our private Bible study. Mutual discussion of this kind is the most effective and profitable method of checking our own individual ideas; it also deepens mutual fellowship in the things of Christ, and it provides a fresh stimulus to continue in the study of the Word, that we may become 'those who, by reason of use, have their senses exercised to discern' (Heb. v. 14).

LIST OF ABBREVIATIONS

Books of the Old Testament: Gn., Ex., Lv., Nu., Dt., Jos., Jdg. Ru., 1, 2 Sa., 1, 2 Ki., 1, 2 Ch., Ezr., Ne., Est., Jb., Ps., (Pss.), Pr., Ec., Ct., Is., Je., La., Ezk., Dn., Ho., Joel, Am., Ob., Jon., Mi., Na., Hab., Zp., Hg., Zc., Mal.

Books of the New Testament: Mt., Mk., Lk., Jn., Acts, Rom., 1, 2 Cor., Gal., Eph., Phil., Col., 1, 2 Thes., 1, 2 Tim., Tit., Phm., Heb., Jas., 1, 2 Pet., 1, 2, 3 Jn., Jude, Rev.

A.V. Authorized Version (1611).

cf. Compare.

Gk. Greek.

Heb. Hebrew.

LXX. Septuagint Version, that is, translation of the Old Testament into Greek, about 250 B.C.

mg. Margin.

Moffatt. Moffatt's translation of the Bible.

R.S.V. Revised Standard Version of the New Testament (1946).

R.V. Revised Version (1885).

Way. Translation of St. Paul's letters and Hebrews by Arthur S. Way.

Weymouth. New Testament in Modern Speech by Weymouth.

INDEX OF BIBLICAL BOOKS

Note.—First Year contains pages 1–144; Second Year contains pages 145–332; Third Year contains pages 333–544.

FIRST YEAR

FIRST YEAR

GENESIS

INTRODUCTION

(See New Bible Handbook, pp. 79-88, 115-133)

THE title Genesis comes from the Septuagint Greek translation of the Old Testament and means "Origin" or "Beginning." The book justifies its title in three ways.

(a) As *history* it tells the story of the creation, of the earliest civilization, of the flood, and of the origins of the chosen people of God.

(b) As *revelation* it teaches primary truths about God and Man: and with regard to the way of salvation it tells first of the coming of sin into the world through the fall; then of the utter failure of early man to save himself, culminating in the flood; and finally of God's choice of one family in which all families of the earth should be blessed. The fact of God's redemptive purpose, first foreshadowed in the garden of Eden (Gn. iii. 15), shines out from time to time with increasing clearness as the book proceeds.

Genesis is thus the story first of man's need of salvation, and then of the early stages in the unfolding of God's wonderful plan of redemption.

(c) As *practical teaching* it introduces us to personalities of profound and universal religious significance, such as Abel and Cain, Noah, Abraham, Jacob and Esau and Joseph, and by its unforgettable stories teaches lessons of abiding value, showing God at work in human life.

AUTHORSHIP

The Pentateuch or Five Books, of which Genesis is the first, was attributed to Moses by universal tradition of the Jews, which our Lord takes for granted and endorses with His own authority, e.g. Mk. xii. 26; Jn. v. 46, 47. This is not the place to attempt to discuss the questions raised by modern criticism, but the following remarks may be made here.

(1) To put the composition of the Pentateuch centuries after the time of Moses means much more than a judgment on its authorship; it inevitably involves surrendering its claim to be

See *New Bible Handbook*, pp. 40-56.

3

reliable history, and, moreover, it involves the unreliability of a great part of Bible history outside the Pentateuch, as the course of modern criticism shows.

(2) There is an important external check on the claim of the Pentateuch to be historical, namely, its representation of the customs of ancient Egypt. Archaeology has shown that these were just such as they are represented in Genesis to be in the period referred to, but that in many respects they had become quite different long before the exile. How could a late writer have attained such accuracy? Not assuredly by archaeological research, which was not dreamed of in ancient times.

Those who desire to study a brilliant exposure in considerable detail of the weakness of the critical hypothesis and of the arguments by which that hypothesis is maintained, cannot do better than read Finn's *Unity of the Pentateuch*. See also Chapter IV of *The New Bible Handbook*.

ANALYSIS

i–xi. Primaeval history.

xii–l. The ancestors of the chosen people. There is some overlapping, but each patriarch is the leading figure within the section to which his name is attached below:

xii–xxv. 18. Abraham.
xxv. 19–xxvi. Isaac.
xxvii–xxxvi. Jacob.
xxxvii–l. Joseph.

Week 1. GENESIS I–XI. 9

Day 1. Gn. i–ii. 3.

(1) Having read the chapter, try to picture the story as a succession of acts or scenes. As you survey these in turn, what truths stand out regarding God and His relation to nature and to man?

(2) 'And God said'—found eight times. Cf. Ps. xxxiii. 9; Heb. xi. 3. What further light upon the mode of creation do we get from Jn. i. 1–3; Col. i. 15–17?

Day 2. Gn. ii. 4–iii. 24.

(1) What does Gn. iii teach about (a) Satan's methods, (b) the first false steps which lead to sin in act, (c) the results of sin?

(2) What prophecy of the Lord Jesus do we find in this section?

Day 3. Gn. iv and v.

(1) Trace in chapter iv the growth of sin and also the evidences of its power and of its effects.

(2) Abel died and Cain lived. But what had Abel that Cain had not? Cf. 1 Jn. iii. 12.

(3) Try to picture to yourself the life of Enoch as told in Gn. v. 21-24. What new light does Heb. xi. 5, 6 throw upon it?

Day 4. Gn. vi.

(1) What do we learn from today's portion of the fallen condition of human nature, of the need of a divine way of salvation, and also of God's attitude to sin? See Mt. xxiv. 37-39; 1 Pet. iii. 20; 2 Pet. ii. 5.

(2) 'Noah found grace in the eyes of the Lord.' What were his characteristics? Cf. Heb. xi. 7.

Notes.—(1) In Gn. vi. 3, the words 'an hundred and twenty years' probably refer not to the average length of human life, but to the respite for repentance which the race was to have from that time to the flood.

(2) The value of the N.T. references is specially great in this portion.

Day 5. Gn. vii–viii. 19.

(1) How long was Noah in the ark?

(2) Once Noah was in the ark, what was God's part in his salvation and what Noah's? See vii. 16, viii. 1, 15, 18. What may we learn from these things regarding our own salvation in Christ? See Eph. ii. 8; 1 Pet. i. 5.

Day 6. Gn. viii. 20—ix.

(1) What did Noah's altar and burnt offerings signify? To what would they correspond in our own life today?

(2) Reflect on Noah's position after the deluge. In what two ways, according to chapter ix, did God encourage him?

(3) How does this chapter teach also the need of *continued* faithfulness, day by day, and that a past experience of the grace of God is no guarantee against present failure?

Notes.—(1) Observe God's care for 'every living creature' (ix. 10, 12, 15. Cf. Lk. xii. 6).

(2) ix. 13. This does not imply that the rainbow was now seen for the first time, but that God now gave it as a token of His covenant of promise to Noah.

Day 7. Gn. x–xi. 9.

(1) What does chapter x teach about the origins of the nations and of their relation to one another and to God? Mt. xxviii. 19; Acts xvii. 26; Rom. iii. 29.

(2) How does xi. 1-9 show the peril of living without God in pride and selfish ambition? What does it reveal also of God's attitude towards all human organization that leaves Him out of account? With xi. 9 contrast Rev. xxi. 24-27.

Week 2. GENESIS XI. 10–XXI. 21

The Book of Genesis passes here from the story of the race as a whole to one line, one family, and finally one man as the chosen instrument of God's purpose of redemption.

Day 1. Gn. xi. 10–xiii. 4.

(1) What light is thrown upon Abram by the fact that such promises made any appeal to him? Consider also the inseparable intermingling of promise and command in God's call and the importance of Abram's obedience, not only for his own life, but in the world purpose of God. See Heb. xi. 8.

(2) Compare and contrast xi. 31 with xii. 5. See also Acts vii. 1-4. On which side of the Euphrates was Haran? Are we ready to cross every barrier and to go the full way with God?

(3) In what two respects did Abram's faith fall short under the tests of famine and of fear? Do you find a special significance in xiii. 3, 4, especially in the words 'where his tent had been at the beginning'? Cf. Rev. ii. 5.

Day 2. Gn. xiii. 5–xiv.

(1) Put yourself in Lot's place when Abram's offer was made to him. What was the motive that decided his choice and how did it end? On the other hand, did Abram suffer any real loss through his unselfishness? Cf. Mt. xvi. 25.

(2) What fresh light do the events of chapter xiv throw on Abram's character?

Day 3. Gn. xv.

(1) Do you find indications in the story that Abram was at this time discouraged? He had incurred the enmity of powerful kings and had refused the spoil of Sodom and Gomorrah. How do God's words in verse 1 exactly meet his need?

(2) See verses 5, 6. Could anything seem less likely to human judgment than the fulfilment of verse 5? Yet Abram believed in the Lord. What great spiritual truth of the gospel does Paul find set forth here? See Rom. iv; Gal. iii. 6-8.

(3) What double ground for faith did God give Abram in verse 7? What *more* did Abram crave and what more did God

give him? See verse 18. The whole chapter is full of God's loving-kindness towards His servant.

Note.—Verses 9, 10, 17 describe an ancient form of agreement or contract; see Je. xxxiv. 18, 19. The smoking furnace and burning lamp represent the Lord passing between the divided animals and thus ratifying the covenant.

Day 4. Gn. xvi and xvii.

(1) Another wrong step on Abram's part brings suffering on others. What attributes of God's being and character are revealed in His dealings with Hagar? See Pr. xv. 3; Col. iii. 22; 1 Pet. ii. 20.

(2) Under what name does God reveal Himself in xvii. 1 and what does He require of His servant? Do you find indications that Abraham at this time needed some such reminder? Consider the strain imposed upon his faith by the passing of the years (xvi. 16; xvii. 1). Notice Abram's change of name in verse 5.

(3) In what respects are God's promises in xvii more definite, more complete, and more gracious than on any earlier occasion? Notice Abraham's prompt obedience in xvii. 23.

Day 5. Gn. xviii.

(1) How do verses 1 and 2 show that 'the three men' collectively were a manifestation of Jehovah Himself? What other evidence do you find that it was indeed 'the Lord'? Cf. Ps. xxv. 14; Jn. xiv. 21-23, xv. 15.

(2) What are the chief characteristics of Abraham's intercession? Can you find at least seven which should mark also our praying? With verses 22, 23, compare Heb. x. 19-22. What did Abraham's intercession effect? See xix. 29.

Day 6. Gn. xix.

(1) What is revealed in this chapter about the evil latent in the heart of man and about the certainty of divine judgment? See Lk. xvii. 28, 29; 2 Pet. ii. 6; Jude 7.

(2) What did Lot gain for himself and his family by his association with Sodom? How does his life warn us?

Day 7. Gn. xx–xxi. 21.

(1) What may we learn from chapter xx of the weakness of human nature, even in a believer, and of God's protecting care? See Ps. xciv. 18; Mk. xiv. 38; 1 Cor. x. 12.

(2) What spiritual lessons does Paul draw from the choice by God of Isaac rather than Ishmael? See Rom. ix. 6-9; Gal. iv. 28–v. 1.

(3) How does chapter xxi illustrate God's faithfulness to His promise both in regard to Isaac (verse 1) and in regard to Ishmael (verses 13, 18)? See Heb. x. 23, xi. 12.

Week 3. GENESIS XXI. 22–XXVIII

Day 1. Gn. xxi. 22–xxii.

(1) Read the incident in xxi. 22-32 in the light of Rom. xii. 17 (R.V.); Col. iv. 5; Eph. v. 15; 1 Pet. ii. 12. What new aspect of God's name was revealed at this time to Abraham? Cf. xiv. 22, xvii. 1; Is. xl. 28.

(2) Reflect on the severity of the test that God gave to Abraham. Notice how often the parental bond is emphasized (verses 2, 3, 6, 7, 16, etc.). See also Heb. xi. 17, 18. Reflect also on Abraham's response, and on the promises renewed to him because of it. See Heb. vi. 11-15.

Day 2. Gn. xxiii.

(1) What is Sarah's character as shown in Genesis? Cf. Heb. xi. 11; 1 Pet. iii. 6.

(2) What features in Abraham's character does the story of this chapter bring out? With verse 4 compare Heb. xi. 13-16.

Day 3. Gn. xxiv. 1-60.

(1) Consider Abraham's servant (a) in his attitude towards his master and (b) in the way he carried through his mission. What may we learn from him regarding our service of Christ?

(2) What picture do you get of Rebekah?

Day 4. Gn. xxiv. 61–xxv.

(1) What light do we get from this portion on the kind of man that Isaac was? See especially xxiv. 63-67, xxv. 28.

(2) Contrast Jacob and Esau, as described in xxv. 27-34, in their habits, character and spiritual outlook. What lesson is drawn in Heb. xii. 14-17 from Esau's conduct in regard to his birthright?

(3) Review Abraham's life. What gives him an outstanding place in world history and makes him a conspicuous example to us all? See Is. xli. 8, li. 2; Gal. iii. 9; Jas. ii. 21-24.

Day 5. Gn. xxvi.

(1) Why did Isaac fail so grievously just after receiving gracious promises from God? What did he not do after this first appearance of God to him which he did do when God appeared to him the second time? See verses 24, 25 and cf. Ps. cxvi. 12-14.

(2) Can you think of any spiritual wells in our day, which were dug by our fathers and which the enemy has stopped up? What can we do to repair those old wells, such as family worship, for example, and also to dig others?

Day 6. Gn. xxvii. 1-45.

(1) Trace the part played by each of the actors in this story. What motive actuated each?

(2) Consider the story in the light of Nu. xxxii. 23.

Day 7. Gn. xxvii. 46-xxviii.

(1) How does the fundamental difference between the two brothers now manifest itself increasingly?

(2) What fourfold assurance did God give to Jacob? Has there been some 'Bethel' in our experience, some conscious transaction with the Lord Jesus Christ, when He declared to us His love and we promised to serve Him?

Week 4. GENESIS XXIX-XXXV

Day 1. Gn. xxix. 1-30.

(1) What evidences are there in this portion of Jacob's exceptional energy and of his zeal in pursuing the object of his desire?

(2) God is not mentioned. Yet in what ways may we discern Him at work in training and disciplining Jacob through the experiences of life?

Note.—xxix. 27 seems to mean that Jacob had to fulfil the week of wedding festivities for Leah; then he received Rachel and served seven more years for her after marrying her. See xxx. 25, xxxi. 41.

Day 2. Gn. xxix. 31-xxx.

(1) Which of Jacob's wives was the ancestress of the Lord? Cf. Pr. xvi. 9.

(2) How does today's portion show the evils of polygamy and supply an answer to the question heard in some mission fields, 'Why should we not have many wives like men of God in the Bible?'

Day 3. Gn. xxxi–xxxii. 2.

(1) It has been said that when inward desire, favouring circumstances and the divine word agree, we may venture forth with sure confidence. How were these three factors present in Jacob's return to Canaan?

(2) In spite of all his cunning and trickery, what qualities in Jacob are to be commended? See especially verses 6, 38-42. How was he superior to Laban in character?

Notes.—(1) xxxi. 42, 53. 'The fear of Isaac', that is, the God whom Isaac reverently worshipped.

(2) xxxii. 1, 2. Cf. xxviii. 12, xxxi. 11; Ps. xxxiv. 7.

Day 4. Gn. xxxii. 3-32.

(1) What is good and what is defective in Jacob's prayer in verses 9-12? Was he relying most upon God, or upon his own resourcefulness? If the former, why was he so greatly afraid? See verse 7; Mk. iv. 40; Is. xxvi. 3.

(2) God wrestled with Jacob at the entrance to the land. Why? Was it that He could not give the land to Jacob *while he was still Jacob*, but only to a Jacob humbled and renewed in heart? How did Jacob 'prevail' in the conflict—by his own strength, or by faith? See Ho. xii. 3-6.

Day 5. Gn. xxxiii.

(1) What is the importance of the title which Jacob gives to God in verse 20? How has he named Him before this time? See xxxi. 5, 42, 53, xxxii. 9.

(2) In the story of this chapter did Jacob behave worthily of his new name of Israel? In what three points especially did he come short? Compare verse 14 (last clause) with verse 17 (first clause); verse 19 with Heb. xi. 9; and verses 18, 19 with his vow at Bethel, xxviii. 22. See 2 Pet. i. 1-11.

Notes.—(1) In other cases of change of name in Scripture the new replaces the old, e.g. Abram to Abraham; Simon to Peter; Saul to Paul. But after Penuel the old name Jacob is found seventy times in Genesis and Israel only forty times.

(2) Jacob's stay at Succoth and Shechem must have extended over several years.

Day 6. Gn. xxxiv.

(1) In this sordid story, which appear the more honourable: Shechem and his father, or the sons of Jacob? How contrary to 1 Pet. ii. 12, iv. 15!

(2) What evidence is there that Jacob left everything to his sons, instead of taking action himself as head of the family? When he did finally rebuke them, about what was he chiefly concerned?

Day 7. Gn. xxxv.

(1) Reading verses 1-7 in the light of 2 Cor. vii. 10, 11, do you find evidence of true repentance in Jacob at this time? In what ways was it manifested?

(2) What new revelation was given to Jacob after his repentance? How does this whole story reveal the loving-kindness and faithfulness of God to His covenant promises, and at the same time His inexorable insistence upon true holiness of life in His people? See Ho. xiv. 4, 9; 2 Tim. ii. 19, 22.

(3) Observe the record of sorrows in this chapter, all of them touching Jacob intimately.

Week 5. GENESIS XXXVI–XLIII

Day 1. Gn. xxxvi.

In chapter x, before the writer concentrates on the line of Abraham, the names of other nations are recorded. In a similar way in this chapter, before any concentration on the family of Jacob, a list of Edom's descendants is given.

(1) It was foretold from the beginning that each of Rebekah's twin sons would beget a nation (xxv. 23), and so it came to pass. Was it the case with the nations, as it was with their progenitors, that the one was chosen of God and the other rejected? See Heb. xii. 17; Mal. i. 2-4; Rom. ix. 10-13.

(2) Jacob and Esau were both sinners. What was the vital difference between them and between the nations that sprang from them? Contrast this chapter with xlix, especially verse 18.

Day 2. Gn. xxxvii.

(1) What three things specially aroused the envy and hatred of Joseph's brothers? To what other sins did their envy lead them? See Jas. iii. 16.

(2) Observe the depths of Jacob's sorrow for the loss of Joseph. Is such unrelieved gloom justifiable for those who believe in God?

Note.—A coat of colours; better 'a tunic with sleeves'. Cf. R.V. mg. It was a garment of distinction, perhaps implying freedom from manual toil. The ordinary tunic had no sleeves.

Day 3. Gn. xxxviii and xxxix.

(1) From what initial false step on Judah's part did all the events of sin and shame in chapter xxxviii originate? What may we learn therefrom? Cf. Gn. xxiv. 3, xxvi. 34, 35, xxvii. 46-xxviii. 4.

(2) It has been pointed out that in Joseph were combined the best qualities of his ancestors: the faith and faithfulness of Abraham, the meekness of Isaac, the ability and energy of Jacob, and the personal beauty of his mother. How is this illustrated in chapter xxxix?

(3) Over what temptations did Joseph gain the victory?

Notes.—(1) In xxxviii. 21, 'harlot' is literally 'holy woman', i.e. consecrated to a Canaanite god; contrast Jehovah's holiness, verse 10.

(2) See Ps. cv. 17, 18, which shows how Joseph's imprisonment began.

Day 4. Gn. xl–xli. 13.

(1) What qualities in Joseph are shown in today's portion? Find at least five.

(2) How did God make Joseph's prison experiences 'work together for good'?

Note.—xl. 2. 'Chief of the butlers' and 'Chief of the bakers' were titles for high officials of Pharaoh's court.

Day 5. Gn. xli. 14-57.

(1) What in Joseph so impressed Pharaoh and his court that he was made ruler of Egypt? What impresses you most in Joseph? When you lay your own character alongside his, wherein do you fail?

(2) If we have found in Christ the Bread of Life and men around us are perishing, what spiritual lesson may be drawn from verses 54-57?

Day 6. Gn. xlii.

(1) What was the motive of Joseph's apparent harshness towards his brethren? For his real feelings see verses 24, 25. Have we not here an illustration of methods which God also uses? See Heb. xii. 6, 11; Je. xxxi. 18, 19.

(2) What brought Joseph's brothers to the recognition and acknowledgment of their guilt? See verse 21.

(3) How mistaken the attitude of Jacob in verse 36! What may we learn from this in regard to our own attitude when 'all things seem against us'? See Ps. xliii. 5; Rom. xv. 13.

Day 7. Gn. xliii.

(1) Why did Jacob yield to Judah's appeal when he had refused the earlier appeal of Reuben in xlii. 37, 38?

(2) Why do you think Joseph gave Benjamin portions five times as large as those given to the others? Was it affection for Benjamin, or was it a further test of his brothers? See xxxvii. 4.

Week 6.   GENESIS XLIV–L

Day 1. Gn. xliv.

(1) How do the actions of Joseph's brothers in this chapter show that they were indeed changed men? Contrast their former behaviour towards their father and towards a young brother in xxxvii.

(2) Observe how in all this second visit to Egypt Judah takes the lead; see xliii. 3, 8, xliv. 14, 16, 18. What qualities are revealed in his speech before Joseph in verses 16-34? And how does this teach us that we should not despair of any? See xxxvii. 26, 27, xxxviii. 1; Ps. cxix. 59, 60, 176.

Day 2. Gn. xlv.

(1) Consider the parallel between verses 1-15 and the story in Acts ii. 22-39. We have, for example (a) Joseph made known to his brethren (cι. Acts ii. 36); (b) Joseph's brethren troubled in his presence (cf. Acts ii. 37); (c) reconciliation following on repentance (cf. Acts ii. 38).

(2) What blessings did the restoration of family harmony and fellowship bring in its train?

Day 3. Gn. xlvi–xlvii. 12.

(1) See Week 4, Day 3 (1). Do you find the same three lines of especial guidance converging in Jacob's going down to Egypt? What larger plan had God in view than was in the thought of Jacob and his sons?

(2) What trait in Joseph is revealed by his whole management of Jacob's arrival in Egypt? See Pr. xiii. 16; Is. xi. 2, lii. 13.

(3) How does this portion illustrate, typically or otherwise, (a) Jn. xiv. 6; (b) 2 Cor. iv. 17, 18?

Day 4. Gn. xlvii. 13–xlviii.

(1) What did Joseph, by their own confession, do for the people of Egypt? How was it that in his exalted position and amid the pressure of secular duties he remained true to his father's God?

(2) Contrast the two retrospects given by Jacob of his life in xlvii. 9 and xlviii. 15, 16. What are the differences between them and which is the one most worthy of our imitation?

(3) Chapter xlviii should be read in the light of Heb. xi. 21. What quality is revealed in Jacob by the fact that, when dying, he 'worshipped' and 'blessed' (that is, conveyed to his grandsons the inheritance promised to Abraham and to his seed)? See 1 Jn. v. 4; 1 Cor. xv. 55-57.

Day 5. Gn. xlix.

(1) Three features characterize this chapter: (a) the unity of the family, cleaving by faith to the God of their fathers and to the promises made to Abraham and to his seed; (b) the sins and blemishes of individuals; (c) the glorious hope for the future. Consider these facts, and note how, because of the first, God in His grace can fulfil the third, in spite of the second. Cf. Ps. cxxx. 3, 4, 7, 8; Mt. xvi. 15-18; 1 Cor. vi. 9-11.

(2) What picture of a victorious fighter is given in verses 23-25a, and what is the secret of his victory? Have you learned this secret? See Eph. vi. 10; Phil. iv. 13.

Note.—Verse 10, 'till Shiloh come', should perhaps be rendered 'till He come whose it is'. Cf. Ezk. xxi. 27, which is possibly an intentional reference to this verse.

Day 6. Gn. l.

(1) Comparing l. 1-13 with xxviii. 10-15, reflect how faithful and gracious God had been in the fulfilment of His promises even in Jacob's own lifetime. See Ps. cxlvi. 5, 6.

(2) Why were Joseph's brothers so slow to believe that Joseph had really forgiven them? What evidence is there that Joseph was grieved by their unbelief, and what light does this cast upon the pain our own unbelief towards God must cause Him?

(3) How long a time elapsed between Jacob's coming to Egypt and Joseph's death, and what was taking place in those years? See verses 22, 23; Ex. i. 7. How does this make Joseph's faith, expressed in verses 24, 25, the more conspicuous? See Heb. xi. 22.

Day 7. Revision.

Consider Joseph as a type of Christ. How many parallels can you find?

LUKE

INTRODUCTION

(See New Bible Handbook, pp. 319-322, 333-338)

THIS Gospel is proved by its style and language to have been
written by a *Greek doctor*, who was identical with the writer of the
Acts of the Apostles, and, as the latter book shows, was a companion of Paul. Only Luke, 'the beloved physician', fits these
conditions, and as he was not a man of note, there would have
been no inducement to attribute the Gospel to him had he not
actually been the author.

The most probable explanation of the abrupt ending to Acts is
that Luke brought that book up to date, and that Paul was still
in his first imprisonment at Rome when Acts was finished. This
would give a date of about A.D. 62 for Acts, and a year or two
earlier as the latest date for the Gospel.

This Gospel lays a special emphasis on the human nature of the
Lord Jesus, though witnessing also with no doubtful voice to His
Deity; see, e.g. x. 21, 22, xxiv. 26, 49. His sympathy with the
suffering and bereaved, the despised and the outcast, is brought
into clear view: and the universal nature of the gospel, intended
for Samaritan and heathen as well as the Jew, is strongly emphasized. The free offer of salvation and the impossibility of acquiring
merit come out again and again, e.g. xv. 11-32, xvii. 7-10, xviii.
14, xxiii. 39-43.

ANALYSIS

i, ii. The birth and childhood of our Lord and the
Baptist.

iii–iv. 13. The preaching of John; the baptism and temptation of the Lord.

iv. 14–ix. 50. The ministry in Galilee.

ix. 51–xix. 28. Journeyings towards Jerusalem; ministry outside
Galilee.

xix. 29–xxi. Last days of public teaching.

xxii–xxiv. The last supper, the arrest, trial, death, and
resurrection of the Lord.

Week 7. LUKE I AND II

Day 1. Lk. i. 1-23. See R.V., especially in the preface (verses 1-4).

(1) What do we learn from the preface as to (a) the sources of
Luke's information, (b) the care which he took to verify his facts,

(c) the importance which he attached to giving a truthful record?

(2) What was the mission assigned to John the Baptist? What was the nature of his greatness (verse 15)? See also verses 66, 67; Mt. xi. 10, 11, 13.

Day 2. Lk. i. 24-38.

(1) Verses 31-33 and 35. What seven things are said in these verses about the person and destiny of the promised Child?

(2) Contrast Mary's reception of the angel's message with the attitude shown by Zacharias. Cf. verse 45.

Day 3. Lk. i. 39-56.

(1) What three divine attributes does Mary extol in verses 49, 50?

(2) What principle of God's working is revealed in the *manner* of the Saviour's coming? See verses 51-53 and 1 Cor. i. 26-31.

(3) What features in Mary's character shine forth in this song?

Day 4. Lk. i. 57-80.

The song of Zacharias may be divided thus: verses 68-70, thanks to God for the coming of the Messiah; verses 71-75, the purpose of the Messiah's coming; verses 76, 77, the mission of John; verses 78, 79, further picture of Messiah's coming.

(1) The song refers primarily to the Jewish nation. On what principle has the Christian Church appropriated it for its own use? See Rom. xv. 8, 9; 1 Pet. ii. 9.

(2) What divine attributes are extolled in Zacharias' song?

(3) What, according to verses 74-75 and 77-79, is the *purpose* of salvation? Who, in the application of the song to ourselves, are our enemies? How much of the salvation here spoken of are we experiencing?

Note.—Verse 69. 'A horn of salvation', that is, one who has strength to effect salvation; the horn of an animal was a common symbol of strength and power.

Day 5. Lk. ii. 1-20. In verses 10 and 14 see R.V.

(1) Verses 1-7. How do these verses illustrate the control of God over all, bringing to pass His own purposes through the free actions of men? See i. 70; Mi. v. 2; Tit. i. 3.

(2) What may we learn from the angel's message and the re-joicing of the heavenly host concerning the *importance* of the birth of Jesus? How are the shepherds an example to us in the manner of their response to the divine word of revelation?

Day 6. Lk. ii. 21-39.

(1) In what ways did Mary and Joseph show their punctilious obedience to God's law? What evidence does the portion give also of the existence among the people of a hidden company of devout souls in whose breasts burned a living flame of pure religion? Cf. Mal. iii. 16, iv. 2.

(2) What did Simeon see in the child that lay in his arms (verses 30-32, 34 and 35)? Whence had the aged saint this insight?

Notes.—(1) Verses 21-24. After the circumcision of the child two rites had to be performed: first, his presentation to God, and redemption by a money payment (verse 23; Ex. xiii. 2, 13; Nu. iii. 44-47); and second, the sacrifice of purification for the mother (verse 24; Lv. xii).

(2) Verse 25, 'waiting for the consolation of Israel', i.e. for the coming of the Messiah. For other phrases of similar meaning, see verse 38 and xxiii. 51.

(3) Verses 34, 35, 'is set', i.e. 'is appointed'. Three things are said: (a) through this child many will fall (cf. Is. viii. 14) and many will rise up according as they reject or receive Him; (b) He will be a sign from God, unwelcome to many; and (c) through Him the secret thoughts of many will be brought to light.

Day 7. Lk. ii. 40-52. Verse 49, see R.V. mg.

(1) What consciousness of a unique relation to God shines out in Jesus' words, and what does He say must be the necessary consequence in His life? How far do His words apply to us, who are sons of God in Him? Cf. Jn. xx. 21.

(2) How does this portion show the Lord's perfection at each stage of His human growth?

Week 8. LUKE III-V. 26

Day 1. Lk. iii. 1-20. With verses 3-6 cf. i. 16, 17, 76, 77.

Verses 1 and 2 show the holy land divided among alien rulers and the high priesthood shared by two men (see verse 2, R.V.). 'What a frame for the picture of the appearing of the Restorer!' (Godet).

(1) What is the Restorer's message? According to his teaching in verses 2-14 neither the forms of religion nor a godly ancestry are of any avail in providing an escape for the sinner from divine judgment. What alone suffices? As regards verses 16 and 17, verse 16 has been fulfilled. How far has verse 17 been fulfilled?

(2) What features in John's character stand out in this passage?

Notes.—(1) Verse 12. 'Publicans', i.e. 'tax-gatherers'.
(2) Verse 14. 'Soldiers'—these were Jewish soldiers, possibly armed police.

Day 2. Lk. iii. 21-38.

(1) What does the 'opened heaven' signify and what is implied in the words 'in bodily form as a dove'? What threefold testimony is given to Jesus by the voice from heaven? See Ezk. i. 1; Jn. iii. 3, 4; Mt. xii. 29, 30; Col. i. 13 (R.V.).

(2) With verse 23 (R.V.) cf. ii. 42. What had Jesus been doing in these intervening years? See Mk. vi. 3. Was He not ready for God's service at twenty-one years, or twenty-five, or twenty-seven? Why did He wait until He was about thirty years?

Note.—An obvious explanation of the difference between the genealogies in Matthew and Luke is that Luke's is really that of Mary, Joseph being son of Heli by marriage; a woman's name by itself would be impossible in a Jewish genealogy. There is no exception to this rule in Mt. i. 3, 5. Notice that Zerubbabel and Shealtiel come into both genealogies: in Matthew, Shealtiel is probably son by adoption of the childless Jehoiachin (see Je. xxii. 30).

Day 3. Lk. iv. 1-13.

(1) What proof do we find in this story that temptation is not sin, and that it may come most strongly after some special experience of God? Observe in verses 2 and 3 the special moment chosen by the devil for his attack. Cf. Mk. xiv. 38.

(2) Jesus was entering upon a life and ministry, the foundation principle of which was faith in, and loving obedience to, God His Father. What light does this throw upon the nature of the devil's attack, and upon his twice-repeated challenge 'If thou be the Son of God'? Cf. iii. 22.

(3) Looking at the three temptations separately, what was the special subtlety of each, and how did Jesus parry the thrust in each case? Cf. Eph. vi. 17.

Day 4. Lk. iv. 14-30. A sabbath day in Nazareth.

In verses 14-44 of this chapter is given a general statement of a preaching tour in the synagogues of Galilee, with a detailed account of two momentous sabbaths.

(1) Verses 16-21. Jesus speaks to the people of His own home town of Nazareth. With what startling claim does He begin, and how does He describe His mission?

(2) Verses 22-30. The people were moved but not convinced. Cf. verse 22. How did Jesus interpret to them their unspoken thoughts (verse 23), and what did He go on to imply (verses 25-27)? What made the people so angry?

Note.—Verses 18 and 19 are quoted from Is. lxi. 1, 2. Note where Jesus stopped: the 'day of vengeance' had not yet begun.

Day 5. Lk. iv. 31-44. A sabbath day in Capernaum.

(1) Try to picture the scenes in the synagogue, in Peter's house, and at sunset. What two facts about Jesus particularly impressed the people in the synagogue?

(2) The reception of Jesus at Capernaum was outwardly very different from that at Nazareth. But was the result very different in the end? See x. 13-15.

(3) Is the theory that demon possession is a form of madness and nothing more reconcilable with the facts here narrated and with our Lord's words and actions?

Note.—Verse 40. The Jewish sabbath ended at sunset. The people waited until the sabbath was over and then brought their sick for healing.

Day 6. Lk. v. 1-11. An eventful morning.

(1) Consider what happened from the point of view of the disciples and especially of Simon Peter: (a) Simon helping the Lord in His work; (b) Simon obedient to the Lord's word in the sphere in which he was expert and against his own judgment; (c) Simon astonished at the Lord's power, and made to feel that he was no fit companion for such a Master; (d) Simon summoned to a new task; (e) Simon and the others forsaking all and following Jesus. Reflect on the change this last step would bring about in their lives.

(2) Consider the incident in relation to Christ's work, and note how it marked a new development. The people were thronging round (verse 3). He needed helpers. How and where did He find them?

Day 7. Lk. v. 12-26. Two outstanding miracles.

(1) Sometimes men doubt Christ's *power* to save, and sometimes His *willingness*. Of which was the leper doubtful, and how did Christ reassure him? What may we learn from this incident in relation to our own need?

(2) Verses 17-26. In how many different respects do you find this miracle remarkable?

Week 9. LUKE V. 27–VIII. 21

Day 1. Lk. v. 27–vi. 10. Various grounds of opposition.

(1) The word 'why' occurs three times in this portion, introducing three grounds of offence which His critics found in Jesus' conduct. What are they, and how do Jesus' answers reveal the principles on which He acted?

(2) The new revelation which Jesus brought raises three questions: (a) Can it be combined with the old? (b) Who are the kind of men to whom the new can be entrusted? (c) What will be the reaction of those who are accustomed to the old on hearing the new? How are these questions answered in the three short parables of verses 36-39?

Note.—vi. 1. This was allowed on other days (Dt. xxiii. 25), but according to the scribes it was not lawful on the sabbath.

Day 2. Lk. vi. 11-38.

(1) Verses 11-19. The excitement of the people was increasing (verses 17-19) and the hostility of the scribes and Pharisees growing more intense (verse 11). What special action did Jesus take? See verses 12 and 13.

(2) Verses 20-38. A picture of the new society of the kingdom of God. Who are welcome to it and who are not? See verses 20-26 and cf. i. 53. What is its basic principle, and in what ways does it manifest itself? See verses 27, 31. How does it exceed the ordinary standards of men, and to what standard does it aspire? See verses 35-38. Are you a practising member of this society of the blessed?

Day 3. Lk. vi. 39-49.

(1) Verses 39-45. If we aspire to be guides to others, what two faults do the two parables in these verses teach us to avoid? Further, on what will our spiritual usefulness depend?

(2) Verses 46-49. When the house of our life is tested, what alone will enable it to stand? Cf. Jas. i. 22.

Day 4. Lk. vii. 1-17. Two outstanding miracles.

(1) How had this centurion come to believe on Jesus? And how did he conceive of Him in relation to the unseen world and its powers? Why was the Lord so astonished at his faith?

(2) Picture the two processions meeting at the city of Nain, and the scene that followed. What features in Jesus' character shine out in this story?

Day 5. Lk. vii. 18-35.

(1) What exactly was the doubt in John's mind? Do you find a clue to his perplexity in iii. 16, 17? Observe how our Lord took him back to the Scriptures (see verses 21-23 and cf. Is. viii. 14, 15, xxxv. 4, 5, lxi. 1).

(2) Note Jesus' testimony to John. If John in his mission was greater than all the prophets, consider how our Lord's words bring

out the surpassing privilege of the 'new covenant' believer. See
x. 23, 24; 2 Cor. iii. 7-11.

(3) What does this portion teach (a) about the longsuffering
mercy of God, and (b) about the personal responsibility of the
hearer?

Day 6. Lk. vii. 36-50.

(1) How did Jesus prove to this Pharisee that it was not
ignorance which made Him tolerate this woman's touch? What
do you think his attitude to Jesus really was? Did he believe in
Him?

(2) What evidence is there that something had already happened in this woman's life and that she was acting under deep
emotion?

(3) What does Jesus look for in those who receive forgiveness
of sins?

Note.—The conjunction 'for' in verse 47 means 'as is shown by the fact that'.

Day 7. Lk. viii. 1-21.

(1) What light do verses 1-3 throw upon the way our Lord and
the twelve were at this time supported? What evidence is there
that Jesus at this time deliberately adopted a new method of
teaching? Contrast the method of teaching here with that of vi.
17-49, and compare Mt. xiii. 11. Note in verse 4 the size of
the crowd.

(2) What experience have you of the truth of this parable in
yourself and in others? What sorts of people do the four soils
represent?

(3) Taking the 'candle' or 'lamp' (R.V.) as denoting the revelation brought by Jesus, what is the application of verses 16-18 to
those who are His disciples?

Week 10. LUKE VIII. 22-X

Day 1. Lk. viii. 22-39.

(1) Verse 25. 'Where is your faith?' Jesus asked. In what was
the disciples' faith defective? Did they not seek Christ's aid?

(2) Verses 26-39. What was the man's condition before and
after he met Jesus? What may we learn from this about our
Lord's power to save?

(3) Why did Jesus grant the request of people who had no
desire for Him, and refuse the request of the man He had saved?

Day 2. Lk. viii. 40-56.

(1) What two kinds of touching the Lord are spoken of here? To what do they correspond in a spiritual sense?

(2) How do the incidents in this portion show the importance of faith and of continuing in faith?

Day 3. Lk. ix. 1-17.

(1) What new development in method is recorded in verses 1-6? Picture the twelve itinerating as here described. What lessons would they learn as a training for their future work and what would be the effect upon the places visited?

(2) What light is thrown in verses 10-17 upon our Lord's unselfishness (the R.V. is clearer here) and upon His concern for both physical and spiritual need? Which kind of need, however, was in His eyes the more important? See Jn. vi. 26, 27.

Day 4. Lk. ix. 18-36.

(1) What was the difference between the popular view of Jesus and that of the apostles? If Jesus were to ask you 'Whom do you say that I am?' what would be the answer of your heart?

(2) What new disclosure did Jesus now make concerning His future path? And what demands did He make upon those who would follow Him? Observe also what claims He makes for Himself.

(3) In the transfiguration scene notice (a) the revelation of Jesus' essential glory; (b) the witness given by Moses and Elijah (representing the law and the prophets) to His death; and (c) the divine approval upon His person and His teaching. In what ways would these facts strengthen the disciples' faith? See 2 Pet. i. 16-18.

Notes.—(1) 'Deny himself' means to refuse to recognize the claim of self.

(2) 'Take up his cross', that is, as those condemned to die were made to do on their way to execution.

Day 5. Lk. ix. 37-62. With verse 42 cf. Lk. vii. 15.

(1) In what five ways, as recorded in verses 37-56, did the twelve (or some of them) fail? Are you failing in any of these ways?

(2) How would you describe the three different types referred to in verses 57-62? Why was Jesus not satisfied with the response of these men to His summons to follow Him? Contrast Jesus' own attitude as described in verse 51.

Day 6. Lk. x. 1-24. The mission of the seventy—a further development in method. See Day 3 above.

(1) What do verses 1-16 show of the passion for evangelism in our Lord's heart (see especially verses 1, 2)? Note also the importance of the message, the responsibility of the hearers, and the principles of divine judgment.

(2) Contrast our Lord's joy in verse 21 with His sorrow in ix. 41. What grieves Him and what makes Him glad? What do verses 17-24 teach concerning (a) the greatness of our privilege in Christ; (b) the Father's method of working (verse 21, R.V.; cf. 1 Cor. i. 26-28); and (c) Jesus' unique relationship to the Father?

Note.—Verses 18, 19. The language here is highly symbolical. 'Heaven', as in verse 15, signifies the height of power and prosperity. The language of verse 19 signifies complete triumph over the powers of evil (cf. ix. 1, 2, xi. 21, 22; Ps. xci. 13; Rom. xvi. 20).

Day 7. Lk. x. 25-42.

(1) What two words show that this lawyer was not a genuine enquirer? How does the whole incident reveal that men cannot escape from the condemnation of the law by whittling down its requirements, which this lawyer tried to do? This was the great mistake of the scribes. Jesus, on the other hand, showed that the law's meaning is far deeper and higher than men thought.

(2) This incident gives the answer of the *law* to the lawyer's questions. What is the answer of the *gospel*? See Jn. iii. 16; 1 Jn. v. 11, 12. Does the gospel exempt men from the obligation to love, or what does it do? See Rom. iii. 31, viii. 4.

(3) With what differing matters were Martha and Mary concerned? Which did Jesus think the more important, and how did He solve the issue? See verse 40, R.V. mg.

Week 11. LUKE XI–XIII. 21

Day 1. Lk. xi. 1-13.

(1) Verses 6-9. Do we not often find ourselves, as Christians, in exactly this position? Someone comes across our path and we feel we ought to help, but we are utterly unable. How does this parable tell us what to do?

(2) How does our Lord's teaching emphasize that it is enormously worth while to pray? Have you grasped the force of His argument, and are you praying? For what supreme gift does Jesus encourage us to ask in absolute assurance of receiving it?

Day 2. Lk. xi. 14-36.

In verses 15 and 16 are recorded two attacks upon Jesus: the one a charge of collusion with Satan, the other a challenge to give a sign 'from heaven'. Jesus deals with the first in verses 17-26, and with the second in verses 29-32.

(1) How does the Lord show the unreasonableness and falsity of the charge that He cast out devils by the devil's aid?

(2) What was the sign of Jonas the prophet? The Ninevites would regard him as one who had almost risen from the dead, and they repented at his preaching. How would the generation to whom Jesus preached stand in comparison in the judgment day, when they refused to repent even when He did actually rise from the dead? See Mt. xii. 40; 1 Cor. xv. 4.

(3) What was wrong with the generation to whom Jesus spoke? The light shone, but they did not see. Why?

Notes.—(1) Verse 19. 'Your sons', i.e. Jewish exorcists. Verses 20-22 show Jesus' complete mastery over Satan in comparison with the imperfect cures of the exorcists in verses 24-26.

(2) Verse 36. Jesus here describes the man who is wholly open to the light as himself transformed by it, so as to become 'full of light'. Cf. 2 Cor. iii. 18.

Day 3. Lk. xi. 37-54.

In verses 39-44 Jesus addresses the Pharisees, and in verses 45-52 the lawyers (or scribes).

(1) How would you translate His accusations against the Pharisees into terms of modern life?

(2) What three charges does He level against the lawyers, and what judgment does He say is on its way?

Notes.—(1) Verse 41. A loving spirit is the true purifier.

(2) Verse 44. Contact with a grave was defiling (Nu. xix. 16). Hence the Jews were accustomed to whitewash their graves that people might avoid them.

(3) Verse 49. 'The wisdom of God', probably meaning 'God in His wisdom'. Cf. Pr. i. 20-31.

Day 4. Lk. xii. 1-12.

(1) In the light of xi. 49, 53, 54 and xii. 1, consider what need there must have been to steady and strengthen the disciples.

(2) What is Jesus' teaching here concerning (a) the final triumph of His word; (b) the security of His people; (c) the final difference between faithful confessors and those who deny or blaspheme; (d) the divine help that will be given in the hour of need?

(3) What, then, should be the inner attitude of the disciple in the face of threatening danger?

Day 5. Lk. xii. 13-34.

(1) In what does a man's life consist? See verse 15 and cf. Jn. xvii. 3.

(2) Where did the rich man in the parable go wrong? Was he wrong to pull down his barns and build greater?

(3) What should be the central motive in the life of a Christian? And if this is functioning rightly, what about other things? Why need not the Christian 'be anxious'?

Notes.—(1) Verse 22. 'Take no thought'; follow R.V.: 'Be not anxious'.
(2) Verse 31. 'The kingdom of God'; see Rom. xiv. 17.

Day 6. Lk. xii. 35-59.

The thought of the kingdom leads naturally to the return of the King.

(1) What exactly is meant by being ready for the Lord's return? What aspects of readiness and unreadiness are shown in the three parables in verses 35-48?

(2) Consider (a) the suddenness of the return; (b) the greatness of the rewards to the faithful; and (c) the principle on which judgment is inflicted on the unfaithful.

(3) Before the return can take place, Jesus must endure the cross which, while it brings salvation, brings also division and judgment. What warning does the Lord give to His disciples about the former (verses 51-53), and what to the multitude about the latter (verses 54-59)?

Notes.—(1) Verse 49. Follow R.S.V. here: 'I came to cast fire upon the earth; and would that it were already kindled!'
(2) Verse 50. The suspense and agony of anticipation are meant; the thought of Calvary was already a Gethsemane to the Lord.
(3) Verses 58, 59. The meaning is 'Be reconciled to God before the day of judgment.'

Day 7. Lk. xiii. 1-21.

(1) What is the connection of thought between verses 1-5 and 6-9? Cf. verses 3 and 5 with verse 9.

(2) Work out in detail the comparison between the woman and the beast, showing in what respects her claim was higher than its admitted right.

Note.—Verses 6-9. Cf. Rom. ii. 4, 5.

Week 12. LUKE XIII. 22–XVII. 19

Day 1. Lk. xiii. 22-35.

With verse 22 cf. ix. 51; x. 1. Note the *solemn* character of Jesus' teaching in these chapters.

(1) The kingdom is here represented as a palace to which

admission may be obtained by entering through a narrow gate. What is meant by this narrow gate (cf. Jn. x. 9), and what is Jesus' answer to the question of verse 23? See verse 24 ('many') and verse 29.

(2) How does this portion remind us of the truth of 2 Cor. vi. 2b, and that opportunities neglected may never return?

(3) Verse 34 is a window giving an insight into the heart of Jesus. What do you see there?

Note.—Verse 33. The three days cannot here mean literal days; perhaps they indicate a definite short period. 'Out of Jerusalem'; outside Jerusalem.

Day 2. Lk. xiv. 1-24.

A vivid narrative of a meal in a Pharisee's house. First, the assembling of the guests (verses 1-6); second, taking seats at the table (verses 7-11); third, Jesus' counsel to His host about the guests he should invite (verses 12-14); and fourth, the remark of someone present, giving occasion to the parable of the supper (verses 15-24). With verse 5 cf. xiii. 15.

(1) What attitude and disposition of heart is commended in verses 7-11 (cf. Mt. xi. 29; Lk. xxii. 26, 27; Phil. ii. 7)? And what in verses 12-14?

(2) What is the connection between the parable (verses 16-24) and verse 15? Notice the 'but' in verse 16, R.V. Were the excuses which the guests made genuine? If not, what was their real reason for not coming? Cf. Jn. xv. 24.

(3) Who finally participated in the feast? Cf. xiii. 29; Acts xxviii. 25-28; Rom. xi. 11.

Day 3. Lk. xiv. 25-35.

(1) Why did Jesus thus emphasize the cost of discipleship at this time?

(2) What, according to verses 26, 27, does discipleship involve? Was this teaching only for the time or is it always true?

(3) How do the two parables in verses 28-32 enforce the wisdom of counting the cost before embarking upon a life of following Jesus? What picture of Jesus do we get from this whole passage?

Note.—xiv. 26. Hate, i.e. love less than Me, especially if there should be a conflict between their claims and Mine.

Day 4. Lk. xv.

(1) What was the occasion of these parables being spoken? And how do they provide a complete justification of our Lord's attitude to the fallen and the despised?

(2) What led the prodigal son to leave home and what led him to return? During all this time how had his father regarded him?

(3) What is the spiritual equivalent of the robe, the ring, etc., when the sinner returns to God? How do the closing verses show that the Pharisees also might have enjoyed all these things, but missed them through a legal spirit? Cf. Ps. lxxxi. 10, 11.

Day 5. Lk. xvi. 1-13.

(1) To whom was this parable spoken, in contrast to the parables of chapter xv? From the fact that the parable gives instruction about the right use of money, do you think there may have been converted 'publicans' present (cf. xv. 1)? There is an almost playful touch in this story, very different from the tone of the next parable spoken to the Pharisees.

(2) For what did the steward's master commend him? And in what way is this steward an example to disciples? See verses 8, 9.

(3) How do verses 10-12 show that Jesus was not in any way condoning dishonest practices in His references to the unjust steward?

Notes.—(1) The *details* of the parable have no special significance.

(2) Verse 9. To be read as in R.V. 'Friends'—perhaps a reference to such people as the 'Lazarus' of the next parable. 'The Mammon of Unrighteousness.' Weymouth renders 'the wealth which is ever tempting to dishonesty'.

(3) Verse 13. A further reason for generous giving, namely, that Mammon, if master, will steal the heart from God. The best way of ensuring that wealth is not master is to give it away with a liberal hand.

Day 6. Lk. xvi. 14-31. The end of a selfish life.

(1) Contrast the earthly scene (verses 19-21) and the scene beyond this life (verses 22, 23). What was the sin for which the rich man was punished? Can you see a connection of thought between this parable and that of the unjust steward?

(2) What does the parable teach about (a) the opportunity of repentance; (b) the reality of future punishment; (c) the authority of the Old Testament Scriptures?

(3) Verse 31. What is the principle lying behind these words? See Jn. v. 36, 38, 40.

Notes.—(1) Verses 16-18. From the days of the Baptist the privilege of the Jew was over; men of every race could press into the kingdom. Yet the moral law stood unshaken as ever, as, for instance, the sanctity of marriage.

(2) Verse 23. Hell: as R.V. shows, the Greek word is not Gehenna but Hades, i.e. the state before the Judgment.

Day 7. Lk. xvii. 1-19.

(1) What four subjects are spoken of in verses 1-10? And what kind of spirit do they pre-suppose in a true disciple, if he is to live according to this teaching?

(2) Study the story of the lepers as an illustration of the way of salvation from sin, asking yourself such questions as 'How did their healing begin? What brought it to pass?' etc.

Notes.—(1) Verse 3, see Lv. xix. 17, 18.
(2) Verse 12, see Lv. xiii. 45, 46.
(3) Verse 14, see Lv. xiv. 2.

Week 13.   Luke xvii. 20–xx. 18

Day 1. Lk. xvii. 20-37.

(1) Verses 20, 21. What do our Lord's words reveal as to the essential nature of the kingdom of God? Cf. Jn. iii. 3; but see also Lk. xiii. 19, and verse 24 below.

(2) What aspects of our Lord's return are emphasized in to-day's portion? How will His return find the world, and how should it find His own people?

Notes.—(1) Verse 21. 'Within you'. The words may also mean 'among you' or 'in your midst' (see R.V. mg.). The general sense is not affected.

(2) Verse 37. Where a society is dead, judgment follows. Cf. Jb. xxxix. 30.

Day 2. Lk. xviii. 1-14.

(1) Verses 1-8. What condition of the people of Christ is implied in the comparing of them to a widow?

(2) The parable is a powerful argument for persistent unwavering continuance in prayer. To bring out its full force, contrast the widow with the elect and God with the unjust judge.

(3) Verses 9-14. How does this parable illustrate 1 Sa. xvi. 7 and lay bare a fundamental error of the Pharisees? What lesson does Jesus draw from it?

Day 3. Lk. xviii. 15-34.

(1) See verse 17. To what characteristics of children do you think our Lord was referring?

(2) What did this ruler 'lack'? And how did the challenge of Jesus bring it to light? Cf. ix. 23, 24; xiv. 26, 27, 33.

(3) What subject filled the Lord's mind in these days, and how did He seek to fortify the twelve in face of it? Looking at today's portion as a whole, what demands are made upon, and what promises are made to, disciples who are willing to go all the way with the Lord?

Day 4. Lk. xviii. 35–xix. 10.

(1) Compare and contrast the two men whose stories are told in this portion. With all these differences what had they in common? What may we learn from the different way in which Jesus dealt with each?

(2) What important part of repentance (in the case of the one who has wronged others) is here shown to us?

Day 5. Lk. xix. 11-28.

(1) What evidence do you find of a growing excitement and expectancy among the people? What was the main purpose of this parable?

(2) What does the parable teach about the present responsibility of every follower of Christ and about future judgment? Cf. 2 Cor. v. 9, 10.

(3) On what ground was the servant who made no use of the pound given to him condemned? Was the excuse he gave for his inactivity a valid one?

Notes.—(1) Verse 14. Observe the hostile conditions under which the servants laboured.

(2) The phrase 'taking up', etc., in verses 21, 22 was probably a current expression for a grasping person.

Day 6. Lk. xix. 29-48.

(1) What was Jesus' purpose in making this public entry into Jerusalem? See Zc. ix. 9. What picture of the nature of His kingship did He give by it?

(2) How does this portion show that love and judgment are not mutually exclusive, as many suppose, and that opportunities for salvation do not last for ever? Cf. xiii. 24-30.

Day 7. Lk. xx. 1-18.

(1) How would a right reply to our Lord's question (verse 4) answer the question of the deputation?

(2) Verses 9-18. To whom and to what does this parable refer? What claim does Jesus openly make for Himself?

(3) Compare verse 18 with Lk. xix. 10. What may we learn by combining these two sayings?

Week 14. LUKE xx. 19-XXII

Day 1. Lk. xx. 19-47.

(1) Observe in what an atmosphere of hostility, intrigue, and suspicion our Lord moved. Consider carefully the meaning of both halves of His answer about the tribute (verse 25). How far are you obeying both commands?

(2) The doctrine of the resurrection appeared to the Sadducee ridiculous, because of the practical complications it seemed to

them to entail. Nor did they find it set forth in the Pentateuch, which they regarded as alone authoritative. How did the reply of Jesus meet their objections on both grounds?   For verse 37, see R.V.

(3) What is the answer to the question in verse 44? See Rom. i. 3, 4.

Day 2. Lk. xxi. 1-19.

(1) What do we learn from verses 1-4 as to how God regards the gifts of His worshippers? Cf. 2 Cor. viii. 2, 12.

(2) Verses 5-19. The divisions are as follows: verse 6, complete destruction of the temple foretold; verse 7, two questions by the disciples; verses 8-19, an outline of what will happen before the temple is destroyed.

What teaching does the Lord give (a) as to the treatment which His disciples would receive; (b) as to their attitude under these trials? What promises does He make to them? Cf. Jn. xv. 18-27. With verse 19, R.V. cf. Lk. ix. 24, 25.

Day 3. Lk. xxi. 20-38.

(1) Verses 20-24. This is the answer to the disciples' question in verse 7. How clear was Jesus' vision of what would happen! With verse 22 cf. xi. 49–51; and with verse 24 cf. Rom. xi. 25.

(2) Verses 25-28. Jesus takes a forward look to His return. Contrast the attitude of Christians at that time with that of the ordinary man. What makes the difference?

(3) Yet Christians also may fail. What solemn warning is given in verses 34-36?

Note.—Verse 32. Some take this verse to apply only to the earlier part of the prophecy, which speaks of the destruction of the temple. Cf. xi. 50, 51. Others take the Greek word '*genea*' to mean 'race' and translate 'this (Jewish) race'; and again others take it to refer to the generation in which the signs begin to appear.

Day 4. Lk. xxii. 1-23.

(1) It is important to keep the different parties and figures in these final scenes clearly in view. Who are mentioned in verses 1-6 and what is the attitude of each towards Jesus?

(2) Comparing what is said of Judas in this portion with the references to him in Jn. xii. 4-6, xiii. 2 (R.V.), 26, 27, can you trace a progressive power of Satan over him? See also Jn. vi. 70, 71.

(3) Jesus, conscious that His death is at hand, discloses that His death is 'for them' (verses 19, 20). What further light is thrown upon the meaning of His death by the fact that He connects it (a) with the passover (see Ex. xii), and (b) with the new covenant prophesied by Jeremiah (Je. xxxi. 31-34)?

Day 5. Lk. xxii. 24-38.

(1) In what various ways does Jesus' love and concern for His disciples reveal itself in this portion? See Jn. xiii. 1. How does He thereby illustrate what He says of Himself in verse 27b?

(2) What root evil, prevalent in the world, does Jesus deal with in verses 24-27? Have you let Him deal with it in your own life? And are you living in this matter after His example?

(3) Can you identify in this passage (a) a special danger to which a backslider under conviction of sin is exposed; (b) the greatest help against that danger; (c) an important duty of the restored backslider?

Notes.—(1) Verse 32. Our Lord's prayer referred not to the denial (He knew Peter *would* deny Him), but to what would follow it. A.V. 'converted' is too strong; read with R.V. 'turned again'.

(2) Verse 36. The command to buy a sword symbolizes the time of insecurity and danger that was at hand: it was not an encouragement to resistance (see Mt. xxvi. 52).

Day 6. Lk. xxii. 39-53.

(1) What great facts about our Lord Himself and about the nature of His sufferings on the cross are indicated by the agony in Gethsemane? Could the prospect of physical pain and death by themselves have appalled Him so? Think of your share in responsibility for that agony.

(2) What is meant by the 'power of darkness'? What other references to the activity of Satan are there in this chapter? Cf. also Col. ii. 15 and i. 13, and consider the bearing of this on the answer to question (1).

(3) What facts show our Lord's mastery of the situation and the truth of His claim in Jn. x. 17, 18?

Day 7. Lk. xxii. 54-71.

(1) Trace out the various stages in Peter's downfall from verses 33-60. What brought him to repentance?

(2) Consider what our Lord had to endure, as described in verses 63-71. Meditate also on His sayings. Especially ask yourself, 'What does it mean to *me* that the Son of *Man* is seated at the right hand of the power of God?'

Note.—Verse 70. 'Ye say that I am', that is, 'It is as you say, I am He.'

Week 15. LUKE XXIII AND XXIV

Day 1. Lk. xxiii. 1-25.

(1) What evasions of duty did Pilate make? We blame him; but if we reflect on what happens still, when people are faced by the claims of Jesus, what analogies should we find? Have you ever been guilty of similar evasions or compromise?

(2) How does this portion illustrate ii. 35b? How did the religious leaders of the Jews, Pilate, Herod, and the crowd show their true inward character and attitude when they had to say 'Yes' or 'No' to Jesus?

Day 2. Lk. xxiii. 26-49.

(1) Verses 26-31. 'In the Via Dolorosa Jesus experienced two alleviations of His suffering: the strength of a man relieved His body from the burden of the cross and the pain of His soul was cooled by the sympathy of women. Is it not a parable—a parable of what men and women can do for Him still?' (Stalker).

(2) What different attitudes towards our Lord are represented among those who were gathered round His cross?

Note.—Verse 31. A proverbial expression, which probably means: 'If the Romans treat one whom they admit to be innocent thus, what will they do to this city, when it rises up in rebellion against them?'

Day 3. Lk. xxiii. 26-49 (again).

(1) Verses 39-43. What brought this robber to penitence and faith? Was it anything that he had seen or heard on the way to or at Calvary? Consider the greatness of his faith, exercised in such surroundings. Notice also how the answer given by Jesus to his prayer far exceeded what he asked. Cf. Eph. ii. 4-7.

(2) What other words of our Lord on the cross are recorded by Luke, and what do we learn from each?

Day 4. Lk. xxiii. 50–xxiv. 12. With xxiv. 5, R.V. mg. cf. Rev. i. 18, A.V.

(1) What do we learn from verses 50-56 as to the attitude of Joseph and the women to the Lord at a time when His work seemed to have failed?

(2) Try to put yourself in the place of the women and imagine their experience on Easter morning. Ought they to have been perplexed (verses 6-8)? Is the Lord 'He that liveth' in your personal experience?

Day 5. Lk. xxiv. 13-35. With verse 34 cf. 1 Cor. xv. 5.

(1) Why do you think the Lord appeared to Peter before any of the other apostles? Cf. Mt. xii. 20.

(2) What do we learn from the story of the two disciples and from verses 44, 45 about the unity and inspiration of the Scriptures of the Old Testament, and about their trustworthiness? Also, what is needed in us if we are to gain in full measure what the Scriptures have to give?

Day 6. Lk. xxiv. 36-53.

(1) What was the first reaction of the disciples to the resurrection, as narrated in this chapter? What proofs convinced them that Jesus was indeed risen?

(2) What are the fundamental facts of the gospel to which witness must be borne 'the wide world o'er'? Who are to bear that witness, and in what power?

Note.—Verse 43. To be able to receive food is not necessarily the same as to need it.

Day 7. Revision.

EXODUS I–XX

INTRODUCTION

(See New Bible Handbook, pp. 89, 108, 115-123, 133-137)

THE name 'Exodus', taken from the Septuagint translation, means 'going out'. If we apply the word 'redeem' to the great deliverance from Egypt (Ex. vi. 6, xv. 13), the book itself shows us in which direction to look for the spiritual meaning lying behind the historic fact. These twenty chapters are indeed full of types: not only Egypt itself and the deliverance from it, but also the Red Sea, Marah, Elim, the manna, the rock, and the life-giving water, to name only the chief examples, all speak to us of spiritual truth.

In these chapters we read:

(a) Of redemption from bondage by power, and from death by blood; two parts of one whole.

(b) Of the love of God: manifesting itself first in compassion for His suffering people, then in action for their deliverance, and in wonderful patience with their faithlessness and obstinacy.

(c) Of the holiness of God demanding consecration, separation and purity, and giving a law which must be observed.

(d) Of the amazing ingratitude of man, despite the countless benefits showered upon him, and of a ready promise (so soon broken) to do *all* that Jehovah commanded.

(e) But also of one man, Moses who, like Abraham and Joseph, lived in the consciousness of God's presence and showed steadfast fidelity and conspicuous faith.

ANALYSIS

i–vii. 7.   Israel in bondage; the call and training of Moses.

vii. 8–xv. 21.   Israel redeemed; the plagues, the passover, and the crossing of the Red Sea.

xv. 22–xviii.   Israel in the wilderness; needs met, despite ingratitude and unbelief.

xix, xx.   Israel at Sinai; the revelation of the majesty of Jehovah; the ten commandments.

Week 16.   EXODUS I–XI

Day 1. Ex. i and ii.

(1) What was the situation and outlook for the people of Israel, judging by human standards? But what four things are said of God in ii. 23-25? And what evidence is there in these chapters that faith was present and operative in some hearts? Cf. Heb. xi. 23-25.

(2) By what varied means from birth onwards was Moses prepared for his life work? See Acts vii. 20-29.

Day 2. Ex. iii–iv. 17.

(1) After considering God's self-revelation in the incident of the burning bush, in the declaration of His Name, and in His promises, how would you sum up God's being and character?

(2) What made Moses so reluctant to accept God's call? Was his attitude to be commended? See 2 Cor. iii. 5; Rom. xii. 3. But why, then, was the anger of the Lord kindled against him?

Note.—iii. 22. A.V., 'Borrow' correctly rendered 'ask' in R.V., so also xi. 2, xii. 35.

Day 3. Ex. iv. 18–vi. 9.

(1) Contrast iv. 29-31 with v. 20-21. What had intervened to

effect such a change in the people's attitude? Consider how Moses must have felt it. In his distress what did he do?

(2) How did God answer Moses' cry? Make a list of God's sevenfold 'I will' in vi. 2-9. If, as He did, He fulfilled these promises to Israel, what encouragement should this give us in regard to His promises to us in Christ?

Notes.—(1) Ex. iv. 24. This seems to mean that Moses was struck down by a severe and dangerous illness, the result of his neglect to circumcise his son, and his life was saved by Zipporah's prompt action. He could not act as God's instrument while in disobedience to His covenant.

(2) Ex. vi. 3. 'Known', R.V. mg. 'made known', i.e. in the meaning of the Name: there was no Jehovah-revelation to them. Once only in Genesis did God use that name of Himself, and then without emphasis or explanation (Gn. xxviii. 13).

Day 4. Ex. vi. 10–vii.

(1) How does God answer Moses' despairing plea in vi. 30? See vii. 1-5, and compare Is. xlii. 13.

(2) On what power did Pharaoh rely in his opposition to God's command? See vii. 11-13 and 22-23. In what form does this same kind of opposition manifest itself now? See 2 Tim. iii. 1-9.

Note.—vi. 12. 'Of uncircumcised lips'—uncircumcision symbolizes unfitness for God's service and hence, more generally, unfitness. Cf. iv. 10.

Day 5. Ex. viii.

(1) What is mentioned in this chapter as the double purpose of the plagues? See also Is. xlv. 22-25.

(2) What new evidences are given of God's power, and how would these hearten the people of Israel?

Note.—Verse 26; a reference to the sacrifice in Israelitish worship of bulls, cows or oxen, which in Egypt were sacred to Isis and therefore sacrosanct.

Day 6. Ex. ix.

(1) How does Pharaoh's attitude show the difference between sorrow for the consequence of sin and true repentance?

(2) What illustration is given in this chapter of the difference between faith in the word of God and unbelief, and of the consequences in each case?

Note.—ix. 15, 16. It is specially important to consult the R.V. here.

Day 7. Ex. x and xi.

(1) What was the result in the life of Pharaoh of persistent rejection of warnings sent by God? See Pr. xxix. 1; Is. xxx. 12-14.

(2) What spiritual lesson may we learn from Moses' refusal to

accept a compromise, where God's command is concerned? See
1 Thes. v. 22, 23.

(3) What was the secret of Moses' great courage? See Heb.
xi. 27.

Week 17.   EXODUS XII–XX

Day 1. Ex. xii. 1-36.

(1) What determined the passing over by the destroying angel
of the houses of the Israelites? And how is this a type of our
redemption in Christ? See 1 Pet. i. 18, 19.

(2) How were the Israelites to use the lamb's blood, and how
its flesh? What is the gospel counterpart of this?

(3) What is the significance of the unleavened bread? See 1
Cor. v. 6-8; 2 Tim. ii. 19.

Day 2. Ex. xii. 37–xiii.

(1) What further aspect of redemption is set forth in xiii. 3, 14,
16? See Lk. xi. 21-22; Eph. i. 19, 20. Are you proving both
aspects in personal experience?

(2) What lessons about guidance are taught in xiii. 17-22?

Day 3. Ex. xiv–xv. 21.

(1) Chapter xiv is one of the most vivid stories in the Bible.
Try to picture what happened, stage by stage. What does the
story teach us about God, about faith, and about the completeness
of God's salvation? See Rom. vi. 12-14.

(2) What does the song of triumph in xv declare concerning
God's character, and concerning what He has done and what He
will do? To what does this correspond in the life of the Christian?

Day 4. Ex. xv. 22–xvi.

(1) What reason is given twice in this passage why God allowed
His redeemed people to suffer thirst, disappointment, and hunger?
Cf. Dt. viii. 2, 16; 1 Pet. i. 6, 7.

(2) In what respects is the manna a type of the Lord Jesus?
See Jn. vi. 32-35, 48-51.

Day 5. Ex. xvii and xviii.

(1) What may we learn from the sequence of the two incidents
recorded in xvii? Amalek was a powerful foe (see Nu. xxiv. 20).
How would the experience at Rephidim strengthen Israel's faith
to meet the Amalekite attack?

(2) What, according to xvii. 15, was the lesson Israel was meant
to learn from the fight with Amalek?

(3) What does chapter xviii teach concerning the necessity of applying common sense to the management of church affairs? And what kind of men should be chosen as rulers? Cf. Acts vi. 1-4.

Day 6. Ex. xix.

(1) Study God's message to the people in xix. 3-6. What does He bid them remember? What does He promise them, and on what conditions? Cf. Tit. ii. 14; 1 Pet. ii. 5-9.

(2) How does this chapter emphasize the holiness of God?

(3) What was the new feature in God's revelation at this time? See verses 9, 11, 19; Dt. v. 22-27.

Day 7. Ex. xx.

(1) What do we learn from the ten commandments as to what God does not want to find in His people?

(2) In the light of Mk. xii. 29, 30; Gal. v. 14, 22, what may we learn concerning the life God does want His people to live and how it may be accomplished?

THE ACTS

INTRODUCTION

(See New Bible Handbook, pp. 344-350)

THE key to the book is found in the opening verses (i. 1-11), where attention is drawn to (1) the continued activity of Jesus, risen and ascended; (2) the apostles as the leaders chosen by Him (verse 2); (3) the Holy Spirit as the source of power; (4) Jesus' programme for the future. These facts are dominant throughout the book. It tells how the gospel spread from Jerusalem—the capital of the Jewish world—to Rome—the metropolis of the Gentile world; and shows also how Christianity, step by step, emerged from within the framework of the Jewish nation to become a universal religion; and these developments are consistently traced to the continued activities of the ascended Christ, and to the working of the Holy Spirit.

ANALYSIS

The book of Acts falls into two main parts: chapters i-xii, which give the story of the rise of the Church in Jerusalem and its extension to Judæa, Samaria, and Antioch; and chapters xiii-xxviii, which describe Paul's three missionary journeys, his arrest in Jerusalem, imprisonment in Cæsarea, and journey to Rome. A more accurate analysis, however, reveals that there are (apart from the introductory paragraph, i.1-11) six divisions or periods, each concluding with a brief summary of progress. We then get the following outline:

	i. 1–11.	Introduction.
1.	i. 12–vi. 7.	Progress in Jerusalem.
2.	vi. 8–ix. 31.	Extension to Judæa and Samaria.
3.	ix. 32–xii. 24.	Reception of Gentiles into the Church.
4.	xii. 25–xvi. 5.	A door of faith opened to the Gentiles.
5.	xvi. 6–xix. 20.	Extension to Macedonia, Achaia, and Asia.
6.	xix. 21–xxviii. 31.	Paul's journey to Rome.

Week 18. ACTS I–VI. 7

Day 1. Acts i. 1-11.

(1) What further preparation for their mission did the apostles receive during the forty days mentioned in verse 3? In regard to what matters were they instructed and enlightened?

(2) What is said in these verses about God the Father, about the Holy Spirit, and about Jesus? The whole story of this book flows from these facts. Are they transforming your life?

(3) What is taught in verse 11 about the fact and the manner of our Lord's return?

Day 2. Acts i. 12–ii. 13.

(1) In the period between the ascension and the coming of the Spirit, what did the disciples do? Note that they made no impact upon the world outside, nor attempted to do so. What difference did the coming of the Holy Spirit make in this respect, and what may this teach us?

(2) What three signs were given in connection with the coming of the Spirit? See ii. 3, 4 and 6, 8, 11. They express in symbol what our Lord had already stated in word (see i. 8), that the coming of the Spirit would lead to power, inspired utterance, and universal testimony.

Note.—Pentecost was the Greek name for the feast called in the Old Testament 'the feast of harvest' (Ex. xxiii. 16) or 'the feast of weeks' (Dt. xvi. 9, 10). It marked the end of the grain harvest, and began on the fiftieth day from the day after the passover sabbath (Lv. xxiii. 15, 16). The season of the year being favourable for travelling, Jerusalem was crowded with Jews from all parts (Acts ii. 9-11).

Day 3. Acts ii. 14-47.

(1) What three passages of the Old Testament does Peter quote and what conclusions does he draw from each?

(2) What twofold offer is made in verse 38, and on what conditions?

(3) Summarize the results of the day of Pentecost. How would you describe the Church of the first days?

Day 4. Acts iii.

(1) The story of verses 1-11 vividly illustrates the gospel way of salvation. Observe how it shows, for example, man's *need*, the method of salvation, and its result. Have you ever been the link between Christ and a soul in need, as Peter was that day? How was the miracle wrought? See verses 12-16.

(2) In addressing these people of his own nation, what sins does Peter charge against them? And what promises does he make to them, and on what conditions? How far are his words applicable to us who are not Jews?

Note.—Verse 13. The word 'Son' (A.V.), 'Servant' (R.V.) is the word used in the Septuagint version for 'servant' in Is. lii. 13 and other similar messianic passages (xlii. 1-4, xlix. 1-6, l. 5-10), and seems to indicate that Peter had these passages in mind. Cf. Acts iii. 26; iv. 27, 30 (R.V.).

Day 5. Acts iv. 1-22.

(1) What caused the beginning of persecution and what form did it take?

(2) Picture the scene described in verses 5-21. Contrast the position, influence, and training of the judges with that of the two apostles. Yet with whom did victory lie? It will be helpful to write out Peter's defence in your own words. See also Lk. xxi. 12-15; 2 Tim. i. 7.

Note.—Verses 1-3. Peter was still speaking to the people when he and John were arrested by 'the captain of the temple', that is, the priest in charge of the temple guards, and by other Sadducees, who were the high priestly party among the Jews. They resented this teaching in the temple independently of their authority, and still more the teaching itself, which was not only contrary to their beliefs (Acts xxiii. 8) but a condemnation of their treatment of Jesus.

Day 6. Acts iv. 23–v. 16.

(1) On what facts is the prayer of the apostles based? And what three petitions did they make?

(2) What were the essentials of the Christian fellowship described in verses 32-35?

(3) What exactly was the sin of Ananias and Sapphira, and what led to it? If such a spirit had spread within the Church, what would have been the result? But what, in fact, did result from the divine judgment upon the sin? See verses 11-16.

Notes.—(1) v. 4. This verse shows that the giving spoken of in iv. 34 was entirely voluntary.

(2) v. 9. 'Tempt'. The word means to put God to the test, to challenge Him, as it were (see Ex. xvii. 2, 7; Acts xv. 10).

Day 7. Acts v. 17–vi. 7.

(1) Verses 17-42 give the answer to the petition 'Behold their threatenings'. Consider in what varied ways God brought help and deliverance to His servants while not wholly exempting them from suffering. Cf. Phil. i. 29.

(2) What purpose did the miracle of verses 19 and 20 serve? Consider its effect upon (a) the apostles; (b) the general body of believers; (c) the people; and (d) the rulers.

(3) How did the apostles deal with the incipient trouble mentioned in vi. 1? What lessons may we learn from their handling of it?

Note.—(1) vi. 1. 'Grecians' denotes Jews who had lived abroad and spoke Greek. 'Hebrews' were Jews of Palestine who spoke the Jewish tongue.

Week 19. ACTS VI. 8–IX. 31

Day 1. Acts vi. 8–vii. 16.

(1) Contrast this persecution in its origin and method with those that have gone before. Why was Stephen singled out for attack?

(2) What was the charge against Stephen? Do you think Stephen may have said something of the kind and that the witnesses are called 'false', not because what they alleged was wholly untrue, but because they twisted Stephen's words? Was not the real question at issue whether or not Jesus is the Messiah?

(3) Stephen goes back in his defence to a time in Israel's history before law and temple existed. Where, in that far-off time, does he find a foreshadowing of the experiences of Jesus?

Note.—vi. 11. Describes a whispering campaign by hired agitators who roused the anger of the people and of their leaders against Stephen, and this led to his arrest and trial (verse 12).

Day 2. Acts vii. 17-43.

Stephen now passes on in his review of Israel's history to the time of Moses.

(1) What does Stephen say regarding Moses as to the time and manner of his birth, his reception at the hands of his brethren,

God's appointment of him, and the services which he rendered? Consider in all these things the close parallel between Moses and Christ.

(2) Ponder the tragedy of Israel's unbelief, as described in verses 39-43. How did it manifest itself first in thought, will, and desire (verse 39), and finally in action (verses 40-43)? What was its penalty?

Day 3. Acts vii. 44–viii. 4.

(1) What two things does Stephen say about the tabernacle and temple, recognizing on the one hand their divine origin, and on the other their inadequacy? Cf. Heb. viii. 4-6.

(2) Consider the likeness between Stephen and his Lord in his life and character and in his death. Whence sprang that likeness? Cf. 2 Cor. iii. 18.

(3) What were the results for the Church of Stephen's witness (a) in suffering, (b) in extension? In regard to (a), see viii. 1, 3, ix. 1, xxvi. 10, 11; Gal. i. 13; and in regard to (b), see viii. 4, 5, xi. 19. May we not say that all the developments, recorded in later chapters, flowed from Stephen? Augustine said: 'If Stephen had not prayed, the Church would not have had Paul.'

Day 4. Acts viii. 5–25.

(1) Measure the greatness of Philip's success in Samaria by the difficulties against which he had to contend. Cf. Jn. iv. 9. To what was his success due? See Jn. xiv. 12; Acts i. 8.

(2) Simon was intellectually convinced of the truth and power of the gospel, but his heart was unchanged. How did this come to light?

Note.—Verses 14-17. The reason, no doubt, why the Holy Spirit had not yet fallen upon the Samaritan believers was that, as this was the first extension of the Church *beyond the borders of the Jewish people*, it was fitting that the seal of the Spirit (Eph. i. 13) should be given through Peter and John, as representing the apostles. In a similar way Peter was chosen to go to Cornelius (x. 5), though Philip was probably in Cæsarea at the time.

Day 5. Acts viii. 26-40.

(1) Consider well this Ethiopian official! An Ethiopian, yet a worshipper of the God of Israel; a eunuch, yet humble and sincere; a man of wealth and position, yet full of spiritual hunger. Does he not rebuke us, who excel him in spiritual advantage, yet fall short of him in faith and devotion?

(2) Learn from Philip how to win a soul. What qualities are here portrayed?

(3) A moment before, these two men were separated by seemingly impassable barriers; a moment after, they are sitting together in absorbed conversation about Jesus Christ. If Christ be not alive and working with His people (Mk. xvi. 20), how could such things happen? But if Christ is alive, may they not happen with us also?

Day 6. Acts ix. 1-16.

(1) What do these verses reveal of Christ's power, majesty, and glory, and also of His compassion, love, and grace? Cf. 1 Tim. i. 12-14.

(2) In what way is Ananias an example to us? Consider what great issues may result from one act of trustful obedience.

Day 7. Acts ix. 17-31.

(1) How did Paul prove his sincerity from the very beginning of his Christian life? Cf. 1 Jn. iii. 14; Ps. xvi. 2, 3 (R.V.); Acts xxvi. 19, 20. What word is twice used of his preaching?

(2) What two marks of healthy spiritual life in a church or individual are found in verse 31? Comparing this verse with vi. 7, notice how the Church has extended.

Notes.—(1) The visit to Arabia of which Paul speaks in Gal. i. 17 should probably be fitted in between verses 21 and 22 of the story in Acts.

(2) Verse 29. 'Grecians', i.e. Greek-speaking Jews, probably the same persons as are mentioned in vi. 9.

Week 20.   Acts ix. 32-xii. 24

Day 1. Acts ix. 32-42.

(1) What evidences do you find in these verses that a widespread revival was going on at this time, and that Christ, dwelling in His people, still moved among men as Saviour, Teacher, Healer, Friend?

(2) How do you picture Dorcas? What ideals of Christian character and service are exemplified in her?

Note.—How reminiscent Peter's words and actions are of his Master! With verse 34 cf. Mk. ii. 11; Jn. v. 8; and with verses 40, 41 cf. Mk. v. 35-43.

Day 2. Acts ix. 43-x. 22.

(1) Contrast the two towns, Joppa and Cæsarea, and the two men, Peter and Cornelius. It has been said that this chapter represents in miniature the whole story of the Acts. Do you agree?

(2) What practical action did their visions involve for Cor-

nelius and for Peter? Are we also willing, on receiving new light from God, to follow Christ along new paths?

Notes.—(1) ix. 43. This verse really belongs to the Cornelius story. Joppa was a very Jewish town, loyal to ancient tradition; Cæsarea a semi-pagan city, modelled on Rome.

(2) x. 1. Cornelius was a Gentile, a Roman soldier of 'the Italian cohort' (R.V. mg.), so called, probably, because composed of men born in Italy.

(3) x. 4. 'For a memorial'. The word is that used in Lv. ii. 2, etc., in connection with the remembrance offering. The angel's message assures Cornelius that though, in his uncircumcision, he had no share in the sacrifices of the temple, yet his prayers and alms were acceptable before God.

Day 3. Acts x. 23-48.

(1) What new truth had Peter learned from the vision? See verses 28 and 35. Are we retaining through prejudice distinctions which God has removed?

(2) When Peter addressed Jews, what truths did he use to awaken their conscience (see ii. 36, iii. 13-15)? What truth did he use now? Do you find any other indications in this address that it was spoken before a Gentile audience?

(3) Consider the character of Cornelius as revealed in this chapter. If he was such a devout man before, what did he gain by believing on Jesus? See xi. 14.

Note—Verses 34, 35. The meaning of Peter's words is not that men can be saved by their own good works, but that men like Cornelius and his friends are not excluded from God's favourable regard on the ground of their nationality. Their devout spirit is just as pleasing in God's sight as a similar spirit and behaviour would have been in a Jew.

Day 4. Acts xi. 1-18.

(1) On what does Peter lay emphasis in his story of what happened? Note, for example, what he was doing when he saw the vision, whence the sheet came and whither it went, why the men came seeking him, and why he went with them. Note, too, the phrase 'the angel standing in his house'. If an angel stood there, might not an apostle do so?

(2) Verse 16. 'Ye shall be baptized'. When the words were spoken by Jesus (see i. 5) the apostles had no idea that any who were not Jews could be included in the 'ye'. But what, in fact, had now happened? This is the climax of Peter's argument, and it leads on logically to the doctrine of Eph. iii. 6.

Note.—Verse 2. 'They that were of the circumcision'—an indication that there was in the church in Jerusalem a conservative party who insisted on the necessity of circumcision for all. Cf. xv. 1, 5.

Day 5. Acts xi. 19-30.

(1) What was the distinctive feature that from the beginning marked the preaching of the gospel at Antioch (see note below)? And what was the result?

(2) What three stages marked the establishing of the church there?

(3) What evidences are found in the story of the vitality and influence of the church in Antioch and of its Christian spirit? Cf. ii. 44, 45, iv. 34-37.

Notes.—(1) Verse 22. The city of Antioch, capital of the Roman province of Syria, was one of the three largest cities of the empire. It was famous for its commerce, art and literature, and infamous for its vice and frivolity.

(2) 'Grecians', better as in R.V., 'Greeks'. What is meant is not Greek-speaking Jews, but Greek-speaking *Gentiles*.

(3) Verse 26. 'Christians'—a name probably given first by the heathen populace, but accepted later as a name in which to glory (1 Pet. iv. 16).

Day 6. Acts xii. 1-17.

(1) What evidence is there in this portion of changes (a) in the government of Palestine; (b) in the mood of the people of Jerusalem towards believers; and (c) in the organization of the church in Jerusalem?

(2) Was ever deliverance so unlikely? Consider how many obstacles lay between Peter and liberty. What was the church's resource?

(3) Can you bear witness that intercessory prayer has not lost its efficacy? Cf. 2 Cor. i. 8-11; Eph. iii. 20, 21.

Notes.—(1) Verse 1. 'Herod the king', a grandson of Herod the Great, who was made king over all the territory ruled by his grandfather.

(2) Verse 6. The deliverance took place on the last possible night and, as verse 18 possibly suggests, in the last watch of the night.

Day 7. Acts xii. 18-24.

(1) How would you estimate the character of Herod from this chapter?

(2) How do these verses show that behind all that happens, God is watching and working? What may we learn from Herod's end?

(3) Review the progress made in this third period. What great new developments have taken place in the forward march of the gospel?

THE ACTS 45

Week 21. Acts xii. 25–xiv

Day 1. Acts xii. 25–xiii. 12.

With the return of Barnabas and Saul to Antioch (xii. 25) begins the story of a great expansion of the gospel among *Gentiles*, from Antioch as a base.

(1) What was the part played by the Holy Spirit in the initiation of the new advance, and in the victory over the sorcerer Elymas?

(2) What was the special significance of the facts recorded in verses 11b and 12?

(3) What evidences are there that Paul now stepped into the place of leadership of the Gentile mission? Contrast, for example, verse 1 (where his name is last on the list) with the phrase in verse 13, 'Paul and his company'.

Notes.—(1) Verse 2. They may well have been praying about the future of the work when guidance came, possibly through a prophet inspired of the Spirit.

(2) Verse 6. Bar-jesus or Elymas was a representative of a numerous class of men who practised sorcery and magic and claimed to control the powers of the unseen world. Their influence was at the time widespread and powerful, as is shown by the fact that a Roman procurator had one of them in his entourage.

(3) Verse 9. 'Saul, who also is called Paul'. The change over, at this point in the narrative, from Paul's Jewish name to his Gentile and Roman name seems to indicate that in Luke's judgment this incident marks the beginning of Paul's special ministry as apostle of the Gentiles.

Day 2. Acts xiii. 13–29.

(1) How does Paul show that the coming of Jesus was the culminating point of Israel's history?

(2) How does he account for our Lord's rejection by the leaders of His own nation?

(3) Contrast in these verses God's grace and Israel's sin.

Notes.—(1) Verses 13 and 14. From Perga to Antioch in Pisidia involves an ascent of 3,600 feet from the sea coast to a high plateau, which at the time was a flourishing region of Græco-Roman civilization. Possibly this was more than John Mark had contemplated when the journey began, and hence his return to Jerusalem.

(2) Verse 16. 'Men of Israel, and ye that fear God'. The synagogue congregation consisted of two classes: Jews and God-fearing Gentiles. Paul, throughout his address, expressly includes both. See also verse 26.

Day 3. Acts xiii. 30-43.

(1) What proofs does Paul give that, notwithstanding His death upon a tree, Jesus is the promised Messiah?

(2) What offer does Paul make to his hearers? And what warning does he give?

(3) What was the immediate effect of Paul's words? See verses 42 and 43 (R.V.). What counsel did the apostles give to those who followed them?

Notes.—(1) Verse 34. A quotation from Is. lv. 3 (LXX), which may be translated 'I will give you the holiness of David that fails not' (Moffatt). That points to an enduring holiness, incompatible with corruption and decay (cf. verse 35.). This was not fulfilled in David himself (verse 36), but has been fulfilled in Jesus (verse 37).

(2) Verse 39. Paul here sets side by side two contrasted methods of justification: the one, by the works of the law, failing to achieve the end desired; the other, through faith in Jesus, introducing the soul into the immediate blessing of full justification. Cf. Phil. iii. 6-9.

Day 4. Acts xiii. 44-52.

(1) Picture the scene described in verses 44 and 45. What bold action did Paul and Barnabas now take, and on what grounds did they justify it? See verses 46, 47. Consider with what sorrow of heart they must have seen the unbelief of their fellow countrymen. Cf. Rom. ix. 1-5.

(2) What results followed the decision to turn to the Gentiles (a) in the wider proclamation of the gospel and ingathering of believers; (b) in the stirring up of persecution of the missionaries; and (c) in the experience of the converts?

Notes.—(1) Verse 49 covers a considerable period, probably some months.
(2) Verse 50. 'Devout and honourable women', that is, women of high social position who had become worshippers of the God of Israel.

Day 5. Acts xiv. 1-12.

(1) Observe carefully the course of events in Iconium. Each verse of verses 1-6 describes a fresh development. Do you notice three main stages in the work?

(2) Comparing the work in Iconium with that at Pisidian Antioch, what points of similarity and what of contrast do you find?

(3) Signs and wonders had been done in Iconium, and were continued at Lystra in a notable miracle. What was the effect upon the people? With regard to gifts of healing and working of miracles, see 1 Cor. xii. 4, 9, 10, 11, 29, 30, xiii. 2.

Notes.—(1) Iconium was a prosperous commercial city on one of the main trade routes from east to west. Hence the presence there of many Jews. Lystra was a smaller and more rustic town, with a simpler and less-educated population.
(2) Verse 1. 'So spake'— possibly for a number of sabbaths.

Day 6. Acts xiv. 13-28.

(1) What five elementary truths about God, suited to a heathen audience, are set forth by Paul in verses 15-17?

(2) In what ways did the apostles seek to strengthen the churches they had founded? What may we learn from this?

Notes.—(1) Verse 19. Cf. Acts ix. 16; 1 Thes. ii. 15, 16.

(2) Verse 21. 'Taught many', better 'made many disciples' (R.V.).

Day 7.

Consider afresh this model missionary enterprise, recorded in Acts xiii and xiv (a) in its origin, progress, and results, and (b) in the character, aims, methods, and teaching of the missionaries.

Week 22. Acts xv–xvii. 21

Day 1. Acts xv. 1-12.

(1) The question at issue was: 'On what terms can Gentiles be saved?' What answer did Paul and Barnabas give (see xiv. 27, last clause)? And what answer did the teachers from Judæa give?

(2) Of what three facts did Peter remind the council (verses 7-9)? And what conclusion did he deduce from them (verses 10, 11)? Try to state the argument in your own words.

Notes.—(1) Verse 7. 'Much disputing'. The discussion may have extended over some days and been marked by considerable heat and fire (cf. verse 2 and verse 12, 'all the multitude kept silence'). Luke records only the closing speeches.

(2) Peter's speech contains in germ two truths which find fuller expression in the Epistles to the Hebrews, Romans, and Galatians. The first is that the Gentiles, in receiving Christ through faith, had received the full messianic blessing, hence law and circumcision were unnecessary (see Heb. viii. 6, 13). The second is that the law had not brought salvation to the Jews, who themselves were saved by faith. Why therefore impose the law upon Gentile believers? The two principles of law and grace—or works and faith—are incompatible (see Rom. iv. 13-16; Gal. v. 2-6).

Day 2. Acts xv. 13-33.

(1) How does James show that God was doing a *new* thing, yet one that was in full accord with His eternal purpose as declared in the prophets? What, then, was his judgment on the question at issue?

(2) What evidence do you find in the whole discussion, and in the decision arrived at, of the Holy Spirit's guiding and controlling? The whole chapter provides a striking illustration of Christian comity.

(3) The bigness of the issue at stake may be seen by asking what might have happened if the decision had been otherwise. As it was, what was the result? See verse 31 and xvi. 5.

Notes.—(1) 'James', the Lord's brother, who, as head of the church in Jerusalem (cf. xii. 17; xxi. 18), may have been presiding on this occasion.

(2) Verse 20. Gentile believers were enjoined to refrain from practices abhorrent to their Jewish brethren.

(3) Verse 21. James seems here to be answering an implied objection, which may have been raised in the discussion, that if the Gentiles were not required to keep the law, the law would fall into neglect. James shows that this would not be so.

Day 3. Acts xv. 34–xvi. 5.

(1) What was the contention between Paul and Barnabas? Which was right, or were both right? Cf. 2 Tim. iv. 11.

(2) What provision did God make for Paul in the loss of Barnabas and John Mark? See xv. 40 and xvi. 1-5.

(3) What great developments took place in this fourth period (xii. 25–xvi. 5)? See *Analysis.*

Note.—Verse 3. Paul firmly opposed the circumcising of Gentile believers, but Timothy in Jewish eyes was a Jew by birth; and it would cause needless offence if he did not wear the sign of his Jewish nationality. Circumcision in itself was indifferent. Cf. 1 Cor. ix. 20, vii. 18; Gal. v. 6, vi. 15.

Day 4. Acts xvi. 6-15.

A new period begins here, recording Paul's greatest missionary effort and achievement: the evangelization of three important Roman provinces—Macedonia, Achaia, and Asia.

(1) By what various means was Paul guided at this time? Trace on a map how remarkable the guidance was, both in what was forbidden and in the final result. What indication does Luke, the writer of the Acts, give that he joined Paul at this time?

(2) Does verse 13 seem an anti-climax after the hopes excited by the vision of verses 9 and 10? Contrast the beginning of Paul's ministry in Philippi with that at Antioch and Iconium, as described in chapters xiii and xiv. Cf. Zc. iv. 10a.

(3) How did Lydia show the reality of her faith? Are we equally courageous and wholehearted?

Note.—Verse 14. Lydia, a native of Thyatira, a city famous for its dyeing. She now lived in Philippi, and carried on a business in purple-dyed garments. She was probably a woman of position and means.

Day 5. Acts xvi. 16-34.

(1) What was the origin of this persecution, and in what way did it differ from all those hitherto recorded? Note the successive stages of it, as described in Luke's very vivid narrative.

(2) What enabled the missionaries to triumph over their sufferings (verse 25) and to remain calm and cool in the midst of terrors (verse 28)? Cf. Heb. xi. 33, 34; 2 Tim. i. 7.

(3) What do you think brought the jailer to ask the question of verse 30? How did the change wrought in him by believing on the Lord Jesus Christ express itself? Cf. viii. 39, xiii. 52; Ps. xvi. 3 (R.V.).

Notes.—(1) Verses 20, 21. Philippi, as a Roman 'colonia' (see verse 12 R.V.), was proud of its Roman connection and privileges. Hence the charges here brought against the missionaries would excite the people and the magistrates.

(2) Verse 22. Read as in R.V. A beating with *rods* was very severe. Cf. 2 Cor. xi. 25.

Day 6. Acts xvi. 35–xvii. 9.

(1) Why did Paul act as he did in xvi. 37? In answering this question consider how different the situation would have been if the missionaries had left in the way which the magistrates proposed.

(2) Verse 40. Who were these 'brethren'? How does their existence show that Paul's work in Philippi was far more fruitful than is here recorded in detail? Cf. Phil. iv. 15.

(3) What resulted from Paul's preaching in Thessalonica (a) in converts, (b) in further persecution? As regards the former, compare Paul's own account in 1 Thes. i–ii. 12; and as regards the latter, how did it arise and what was its method and issue?

Notes.—(1) Thessalonica was the metropolis and most populous city of Macedonia, a centre for both inland and maritime trade.

(2) Verses 6 and 7. Revolution and treason—a subtle and dangerous charge!

(3) Verse 9. 'Taken security'. Probably in the form of a deposit of money, to be forfeited if there was any disturbance.

Day 7. Acts xvii. 10–21.

(1) 'Immediately—by night'. Were the missionaries then in great peril? See verses 13, 14 below. The persecuting malice and hatred of the Jews in Thessalonica seems to have been specially bitter. Cf. 1 Thes. ii. 15, 16.

(2) How are those who attended the Jewish synagogue in Berea described, and why are they commended? Is this spirit and attitude any less rare today?

(3) What stirred Paul to action in Athens, even though he was alone? And what two methods did he use? Nothing is said of any

result from his synagogue ministry, but what came out of the other kind of witness in which he engaged?

Notes.—(1) Verse 14. Read as in R.V.

(2) Verse 17. 'The market'—the famous Agora, the chief place of concourse in Athens.

(3) Verse 19. 'Areopagus', meaning the Hill of Ares; the name of a hill where, according to legend, the god Ares (in Latin, Mars) was once tried by a council of twelve gods. It became the meeting place of an important council of citizens called 'The Council of the Areopagus', but there is evidence that this became shortened to 'the Areopagus' and that the council later met in a building in the Agora. If this is so, Paul did not speak on the hill as A.V. indicates (verse 22), but before the council in the building where they assembled.

Week 23. ACTS XVII. 22–XX.

Day 1. Acts xvii. 22-34.

(1) How do Paul's sympathy and tact appear in the opening words of his speech?

(2) What does Paul say about God (a) in relation to the universe, and (b) in relation to man? And how does he show the error of idol temples, sacrifices, and images in the light of these truths?

(3) What then does he say is the present duty of man, and why?

Notes.—(1) Verses 22, 23 should be read as in R.V. So also verse 30.

(2) Verse 34. 'Dionysius the Areopagite', that is, a member of the Council of the Areopagus, and consequently a man of high position and influence.

Day 2. Acts xviii. 1-17.

(1) Try to put yourself in imagination in Paul's place as he entered Corinth alone. Had ever any missionary a harder task? How did he find a home, a means of maintaining himself, and an opportunity for preaching? As to his inward feelings, see 1 Cor. ii. 3.

(2) What distinct stages can you trace in Paul's work in Corinth? What encouragements came to him, and what hindrances did he encounter?

Notes.—The city of Corinth was the capital of the province of Achaia, and one of the greatest cities in the empire. It was famous for commerce and learning, but also infamous for its wickedness. Cf. 1 Cor. vi. 9-11.

Day 3. Acts xviii. 18-28.

(1) Consider with the aid of a map what long journeys are recorded in verses 18-23. They must have occupied many months. What various ministries did Paul undertake during this time, and what purposes did they serve?

(2) What was Apollo's life story, as indicated here? What were his special gifts, and what three characteristics are noted regarding his preaching? Have you a desire to be mighty in the Scriptures?

(3) How did Aquila and Priscilla help Apollos, and with what result? What may we learn from their action as to our attitude to those who are earnest, but have not had the full gospel set before them?

Note.—(1) Verse 18. 'He had a vow'. It is not known why Paul made a vow. The practice was, however, common among the Jews.

(2) Verse 22. 'Gone up', that is, to Jerusalem. Cf. verse 21.

(3) Verse 25. 'Diligently', better as in R.V. 'carefully', that is, with care and accuracy.

Day 4. Acts xix. 1-20.

(1) What twofold difference between John's baptism and Christian baptism is brought out in verses 1-7? Have you entered into the full heritage offered in Christ?

(2) What methods did Paul use in Ephesus? And what special incident led to a great victory for Christ? What was the effect (a) on the people; (b) on believers; (c) on those who practised magic?

(3) Consider the great results achieved in Ephesus and in the whole period from xvi. 6 to xix. 20. By what power were they wrought? See xvi. 14, xviii. 9, xix. 11, 20.

Notes.—(1) Ephesus was the metropolis of the large and wealthy province of Asia, a centre of commerce and religion, and famous also for its magic. Cf. verses 18, 19 (R.V. mg.).

(2) Verse 2. Read as in R.V.

(3) Verse 9. 'The school of Tyrannus', probably the lecture hall of some pagan teacher.

(4) Verse 10. 'All they that dwelt in Asia'—the province was evangelized. The seven churches of Asia mentioned in Rev. i were probably among those founded at this time.

(5) Verses 13 and 14. Read as in R.V.

Day 5. Acts xix. 21-41.

(1) What were Paul's plans for the future? Whither was his eye turned? But what two things must first be done? Cf. Rom. xv. 19, 23, 24.

(2) How did persecution suddenly arise? What was its cause, and how was it quieted?

(3) What witness is borne by this story to the success of Paul's work and to the influence which he exerted, and also to the cost of missionary service? Cf. 2 Cor. i. 8-11.

Notes.—(1) Verse 24. 'Silver shrines of Diana' (r.v.). The Ephesians were very proud of their temple to the goddess Diana, and of the image of the goddess within it (verses 27, 35). Small shrines containing her statue provided a lucrative trade.

(2) Verse 31. 'The chief of Asia' or 'Asiarchs' (r.v. mg.), high officials of the province.

(3) Verse 33. It would seem that the Jews were afraid that the excited populace would turn against them, and sought to exculpate themselves.

Day 6. Acts xx. 1-16.

(1) What was Paul's original plan? See xix. 21. How was it modified, and why?

(2) Try to picture yourself in the church gathering depicted in verses 7-12, and follow what was done, step by step. Do you find the same spirit in these Gentile believers as that in the first Jewish believers, as described in ii. 42?

(3) What qualities are revealed in Paul throughout this whole section? Cf. 1 Thes. ii. 7, 8; 2 Cor. xi. 28; Rom. xv. 18, 19.

Notes.—(1) Verse 2. This tour in Macedonia lasted probably several months. Paul had not revisited the churches in that province since their founding.

(2) Verse 3. Paul was about to board a vessel sailing for Syria, when it was revealed to him that the Jews had a plot to kill him, probably on board the vessel.

(3) Verse 4. These were doubtless delegates from the Gentile churches, bearing the money raised for the poor in the church in Jerusalem. See Rom. xv. 24-27.

Day 7. Acts xx. 17-38.

(1) How does this address to the elders of the church in Ephesus confirm and add to your answer to question (3) of yesterday? As you measure your outward service and inward spirit against Paul's, in what respects especially do you feel you come short?

(2) What counsel does Paul give those to whom God has given positions of leadership how they may guard the flock against the dangers that threaten?

(3) Have you begun to find in experience the truth of our Lord's words quoted at the end of the address?

Week 24. ACTS XXI–XXV. 12
Day 1. Acts xxi. 1-16.

(1) Follow this voyage on a map. Picture especially the moving scene in verse 5. What a memory for the children through life!

(2) How are we to understand these warnings of the Spirit? To Paul's friends they seemed to say 'Do not go to Jerusalem', but Paul himself did not so interpret them. Is the explanation

perhaps this: that the Spirit gave clear warning of peril and suffering, and Paul's friends, in their human affection, interpreted this in one way, while Paul regarded it in another and deeper way? Cf. xx. 23, 24; Mt. xvi. 21-23.

Note.—Verses 15, 16. Read as in R.V. Cæsarea was sixty-four miles from Jerusalem. The meaning seems to be that the party rested for a night on the way at the house of Mnason, who was one of the early disciples.

Day 2. Acts xxi. 17-36.

(1) It was Paul's hope and desire that a closer unity of spirit might be established between the church in Jerusalem and the Gentile churches. What initial difficulty did James and the elders feel must be removed, and how did they suggest it might be dealt with?

(2) In verse 14 Paul refused to yield to the counsel of friends. In this case he yielded willingly. What was the principle that determined his action in both cases? See xx. 24; 1 Cor. ix. 20-23, x. 32, 33.

(3) What happened? Try to picture the vividly described scene.

Note.—Verse 23. 'We have four men'. These men were Jewish Christians who were about to complete a Nazirite vow by offering the prescribed sacrifices (see Nu. vi. 13-21). It was considered a meritorious act to defray the expenses of poor Nazirites.

Day 3. Acts xxi. 37-xxii. 21.

(1) As you consider the circumstances under which this speech of Paul was made, what impresses you most in regard to it?

(2) What was Paul's main aim, and how do the different parts of his speech contribute to it?

(3) What practical lessons may we learn from the fact that, in spite of Paul's arguments in verses 19, 20, the Lord gave him the command in verse 21?

Day 4. Acts xxii. 22–xxiii. 10.

(1) In Philippi Paul allowed himself to be scourged, and only later mentioned the fact of his Roman citizenship. Why did he act otherwise in this instance? In what respect were the circumstances different?

(2) How did Paul twice attempt to get a hearing before the Jewish council when he was brought there by the Roman chief captain, and how was he foiled on each occasion?

Notes.—(1) xxii. 26. It was one of the privileges of Roman citizens that they were exempt from the punishment of scourging. If the chief captain had scourged a citizen of Rome he would have put himself seriously in the wrong. Cf. verse 29.

(2) xxiii. 1. 'Lived', literally 'lived as a citizen'. Paul's meaning was 'Men and brethren, I have fulfilled my duty to the commonwealth of Israel in all good conscience, in the sight of God, until this day'

(3) xxiii. 5. This was not a formal meeting of the Jewish Council, at which the high priest was presiding, but a meeting summoned by the chief captain and no doubt presided over by himself. Paul therefore did not know that the voice that spoke was that of the high priest.

Day 5. Acts xxiii. 11-35.

(1) Consider how greatly Paul must have needed comfort and cheer (a) because of the physical strain he had undergone; (b) because of the pain of Israel's unbelief; (c) because of the seeming failure of his witness; and (d) because of the danger that he was to become aware of next day. How would the vision and the words spoken by the Lord meet all these needs?

(2) God sends deliverance in many different ways. How did He send deliverance in this case? Think how much it must have meant to Paul to have this touch of human kindness amid the sea of hatred that surrounded him, and consider how true is the saying 'Man is immortal till his work is done', as illustrated in Paul's life.

Day 6. Acts xxiv. 1-21.

(1) The Jewish prosecution employed on this occasion a trained advocate. What four charges were brought against Paul?

(2) Notice in Paul's defence what answer he gave to each charge: to the first and second in verses 11-13, to the third in verses 14-16, and to the fourth in verses 17, 18.

(3) What three things does Paul assert in verses 14-16 concerning the Christian faith (a) in its relation to the Scriptures; (b) in its hope concerning the future; and (c) in its effect upon the personal life and character of those who practise it?

Notes.—(1) Verse 8. In the A.V. the preposition 'whom' refers to Lysias, but in the R.V. to Paul.

(2) Verse 18. 'Purified'. Cf. 'profane', verse 6.

(3) Verses 19-21. Paul ends on a strain of irony. 'These' (pointing to his accusers) 'cannot witness to what I did in the temple, for they were not there. All they know is what I did at the council meeting. Are they accusing me of declaring my faith in the resurrection of the dead?'

Day 7. Acts xxiv. 22–xxv. 12.

(1) Why did Felix not acquit Paul? What may we learn from his behaviour of the peril of putting off doing right because it is inconvenient?

(2) Notice how 'righteousness, self-control, and judgment to come' are part of 'the faith in Christ'. Does your presentation of the gospel to others include these elements?

(3) Why did Paul refuse Festus' offer for a trial in Jerusalem, and instead, as a Roman citizen, claim his right of appeal to Cæsar? See verses 9 and 10; also verse 3.

Week 25. ACTS XXV. 13–XXVIII

Day 1. Acts xxv. 13-27.

(1) How would you describe Festus, as seen by his words and actions in this chapter? In what is he to be commended? And wherein did he fail, like Pilate and Felix before him? Cf. Mk. xv. 15; Acts xxiv. 27, xxv. 9.

(2) Taking the Lord's words in xxiii. 11 as the key to Paul's experiences at this time, while to human judgment he might seem a friendless and unwanted outcast, tossed to and fro between Jew and Roman, in reality before what various important persons and audiences did he fulfil his rôle as a witness to Jesus Christ? Cf. ix. 15, 16, xxii. 15.

Day 2. Acts xxvi. 1-23.

(1) In his defence Paul answers three questions: (a) What was he before his conversion (see especially verses 5 and 9)? (b) How did his conversion come about? (c) What did he do after his conversion, and why?

(2) The real question at issue was, Is Jesus the Christ? How does Paul's witness help to answer that question? Can his conversion and after-life be explained on any other ground?

(3) How does the Lord, in the commission He gave to Paul (verses 16-19), describe (a) the lost condition of mankind; (b) the content of salvation; (c) the method of salvation?

Notes.—(1) Verse 6. 'The hope of the promise', etc., i.e. the hope of the Messiah and His kingdom.

(2) Verse 18. 'By faith in Me'; words giving the essential condition by which the whole process described in this verse is to be achieved. The full force of the phrase is 'by the faith, which has Me for its object'.

Day 3. Acts xxvi. 24–xxvii. 8.

(1) The challenge and invitation of the gospel came to Felix (xxiv. 24, 25), Festus, and Agrippa, and was rejected by all. It had come also to Paul, and was accepted (xxvi. 19). What did he gain and what did they lose? Cf. verse 29.

(2) Follow the voyage on a map. What encouragements did Paul receive in the early part of the journey? Who were with him?

Notes.—(1) Verse 24. Paul had not concluded his speech when Festus interrupted him.

(2) Verse 28. The R.V. should be followed here. Agrippa sought to turn the edge of Paul's thrust by raillery.

(3) xxvii. 3. 'Unto his friends', i.e. the Christians at Sidon. Cf. xxiv. 23.

Day 4. Acts xxvii. 9-44.

(1) What were the outstanding events of the voyage, as Luke describes it? The passage should be read in R.V.

(2) When human skill and energy had done their utmost (see verse 20), what did faith do? What may we learn about faith as we see it exemplified here in Paul? On what does it rest? What does it give to him who has it? How does it work? Cf. Is. xl. 29-31.

(3) Life on shipboard, particularly in time of danger, reveals the true character of men. What spirit did the sailors show, and what the soldiers? How did Paul stand the test? And to what was it due that he, a prisoner, became the leader and deliverer of all on board?

Note.—Verse 9. 'The fast', i.e. the day of atonement, which came in the latter part of September and was considered by the Jews as marking roughly the close of the safe season for sea travel.

Day 5. Acts xxviii. 1-16.

(1) What evidences of the Lord's activity do you find in these verses—watching over His servant, opening for him opportunities of service, and giving him inward encouragement?

(2) 'So we came to Rome' (verse 14, R.V.)—triumphant words. Cf. xix. 21, xxiii. 11; Rom. i. 13, xv. 22, 23; also Ps. cvii. 29-31. Has God set some goal before you, and as you pursue the way (it may be a devious one) by which He is leading you to it, are you seeking to help those around you, as Paul did?

Notes.—(1) Verse 2. 'The barbarous people': not 'barbarians' in the modern sense, but non-Greek-speaking.

(2) Verse 15. 'The market of Appius' (R.V.), a town forty-three miles from Rome. 'The three Taverns', a large village thirty-three miles from Rome.

(3) Verse 16. 'The soldier that guarded him' (R.V.), who was bound to him by a chain (see verse 20; Eph. vi. 20, R.V. mg.).

Day 6. Acts xxviii. 17-31.

(1) What was Paul's chief concern on reaching Rome?

(2) What was Paul's message to the Jews in Rome? And what reason does he give for the persistence of so many in unbelief?

(3) In what seven facts does Luke summarize Paul's ministry as a prisoner in Rome? See verses 30 and 31.

Day 7. Acts xix. 21–xxviii. Revision.

(1) Consider more closely the inner spirit of the apostle, as revealed in such passages as xx. 18-35, xxi. 13, 14, xxiii. 1, xxiv. 16, xxvi. 19-23, 29, xxvii. 22-25. What qualities in him are outstanding?

(2) There is a close parallel which extends even to points of detail between Paul's sufferings in this period and those of the Lord Himself. How many such can you trace? Cf. Col. i. 24.

EXODUS XXI-XL—LEVITICUS

INTRODUCTION

(See New Bible Handbook, pp. 115-123, 133-142)

THIS section is sometimes considered by those who first come to it as uninteresting and unprofitable. Readers are anxious to pass on to the narrative portions of the Book of Numbers.

It will be our chief object in this study to find the key that turns these chapters from a dull list of laws that seem to have little practical or devotional interest to living words radiant with the picture of the Saviour. The Lord Jesus Christ is the key to these chapters. While this is true of the whole Bible, we shall find in this section some of the clearest and most poignant pictures of the Saviour and of His suffering for us, definitions of holiness not less plain because expressed in vivid type rather than in direct language, and a concise summary of the great principles and doctrines of atonement. As soon as we understand the spiritual principles that lie behind these chapters they become transformed for us into one of the most precious and wonderful of all sections of the Old

Testament. They draw out our hearts to the Saviour, they fill us
with reverence for the holiness of God, and they become power-
fully influential in inducing within us that separation from sin and
all its ways that is necessary in order that our lives may please
God.

We should note carefully the context of this section. Although
the twentieth chapter of the Book of Exodus divides the book into
two distinct parts, we must remember that the book is really one.
The narrative of the opening chapters leads up to the law-giving
of the later ones, and is bound to it with an intimate connection.
When our section opens, Israel is encamped at the foot of Sinai.
Behind them are the great experiences of God's judgments upon
Egypt, the passover, the passage of the Red Sea, and the wilderness
journey. 'Not a hoof' was 'left behind' (Ex. x. 26). This was a
great separation preparatory to a great santification. The whole
book rings with the note of holiness. God had delivered Israel
from bondage and separated them from Egypt, that He might call
them to Himself and make known His will to them. And these
things are an allegory. God has called us from the bondage
of sin and the world, redeemed us with the precious blood of
Christ, baptized us with His Holy Spirit, and separated us unto
Himself. Israel met with God on Sinai. We have met with Him,
too, not among the thunders of the law, but in the face of Jesus
Christ. Holiness is His intention for us, as it was for them.

The Immediate Context

The voice of God had proclaimed the ten commandments from
Sinai (Ex. xx. 1-17). On account of the people's fear they fled
from the mountain (xx. 18, 19) and asked that Moses should tell
them God's commands. Moses therefore went up into the mountain (xx. 21, 22), and the words of chapter xxi—where our section
begins—are the words of God spoken to Moses alone on the mountain, with the command that he is to pass them on to the people.

ANALYSIS

Exodus.

xxi–xxiii. 13. Civil and criminal laws.
xxiii. 14-33. Various religious laws and promises.
xxiv. Making of the covenant.
xxv–xxxi. Directions for making the tabernacle and for
its worship.
xxxii–xxxiv. The people's sin and its forgiveness.
xxxv–xl. Making of the tabernacle.

Leviticus.

i–vii.	The offerings.
viii–x.	Consecration of the priests.
xi–xv.	Laws of cleansing.
xvi.	Day of atonement.
xvii–xxii.	Various laws as to ceremonial and social purity.
xxiii–xxv.	Laws of sabbaths, jubilee, etc.
xxvi.	Blessings and curses and their condition.
xxvii.	Redemption.

Week 26. Exodus xxi–xxix

Day 1. Ex. xxi. 1-32.

The laws in this portion concern relations between human persons, particularly those between slaves and masters. While slavery is tolerated, its severity is mitigated in various ways.

(1) What kind of relationship between slave and master is contemplated in verses 2-6? See further Dt. xv. 12-18; also Je. xxxiv. 12-17, where is seen God's displeasure at the transgression of this law. With verses 5, 6 cf. 2 Cor. v. 14, 15.

(2) For what kinds of transgression was the death penalty to be surely inflicted? See also xxii. 18-20, xxxi. 15.

(3) If a person be wronged, what does *justice* demand? But if *love* reign, what will the wronged person do? See Mt. v. 38-48.

Note.—xxi. 6. 'Judges'. The Hebrew word is Elohim, as also in xxii. 9, 28. Cf. Dt. i. 16. 'Judges' in xxi. 22 is a different word.

Day 2. Ex. xxi. 33–xxiii. 19.

The laws in xxi. 33-xxii. 15 relate mainly to questions of property, and the remainder of the portion contains miscellaneous precepts.

(1) What instances of careless neglect, leading to injury or loss for other people, are given in xxi. 33–xxii. 15, and what does God demand of the offender in such cases?

(2) Gather out from xxii. 16–xxiii. 19 illustrations of the claims God makes for Himself at the end of xxii. 27 and in xxiii. 7. Against what sin does He say that His wrath will wax hot?

Note.—Some of these laws are similar to those found in the famous Code of Hammurabi,[1] but the provisions are much more merciful. Notice in xxii. 31 the reference to being 'holy men'. Cf. xix. 6.

[1] See *New Bible Handbook*, pp. 136, 137.

Day 3. Ex. xxiii. 20–xxiv.

(1) What does God promise to His people in xxiii. 20-23, and what does He require of them? Can you think of corresponding spiritual promises made to us in Christ and of requirements still more searching? For a somewhat parallel New Testament passage, see 2 Pet. i. 2-11.

(2) xxiv. Why was this day significant in Israel's history? See verse 8, and cf. Heb. ix. 18-20.

(3) Consider the symbolism by which the covenant was ratified in the light of Heb. ix. 19-22. To what measure of nearness to God did it lead? See Ex. xxiv. 9-18. How immeasurably greater our privileges in Christ (Heb. x. 19-22)! But are we entering into them as fully as did the elders of Israel into theirs that day?

Day 4. Ex. xxv.

(1) From where was God speaking and in what form had He hitherto been present with the children of Israel? See xiv. 19, xxiii. 23. What change does He now propose to make? See verse 8 and xxix. 45, 46. How have we in Christ something far better still?

(2) Deduce from the words 'sanctuary', 'meet', 'commune' the purpose for which the tabernacle was designed.

(3) Note the three articles of furniture described in this chapter, but observe specially the ark and what is said of it in verses 20, 22. What is the significance of the fact that only above the mercy seat could God and man meet and commune together? See 1 Jn. ii. 1, 2.

Note.—The 'mercy seat' or propitiatory covering was a slab of pure gold, with cherubim at either end, covering the tables of testimony in the ark.

Day 5. Ex. xxvi and xxvii.

(1) xxvi. What four layers of curtains covered the tabernacle? What appearance would it have from without and what from within? Compare the contrast between Christ seen from without (Is. liii. 2) and seen from within (Phil. iii. 8).

(2) What was the purpose of the veil (spoken of in verses 31-33), and what is its typical significance? See Heb. ix. 7, 8, x. 19; Mk. xv. 38.

Note.—It will be helpful to draw a ground plan of the tabernacle so far as it has been described in these two chapters, with the court, the holy place, and the most holy place, and the altar, table of shewbread, candlestick and ark in their proper positions.

Day 6. Ex. xxviii. The priest's garments.

(1) (a) Who may minister in this tabernacle? Any Israelite? See verse 1 and Heb. v. 4. (b) Notice the phrase 'Aaron and his sons with him . . . that *he* may minister' (verse 1). Of what is this family priesthood, united in one head—he ministering and the rest only assistants—a type? See 1 Pet. ii. 5. (c) Aaron must wear 'holy garments' (verse 2). Why? See the word 'sanctify' (i.e. 'set apart') in verse 3, R.V., also verse 41.

(2) A description of the high priest's garments is given in this portion. For the order in which they were put on, see Lv. viii. 7-9. Each is significant—the coat of pure linen (verse 39) indicating the high priest as a righteous man; the blue robe (verses 31-35) as a heavenly man; the ephod with the names of the tribes (verses 3-29) as a representative man; the mitre with its golden plate (verses 36-38) as a holy man. Reflect how in all these ways the high priest of Israel in his priestly garments was a type of Christ.

Notes.—(1) The Ephod was a shoulder garment, covering breast and back.

(2) The breastplate was probably a bag or pouch fastened to the front of the Ephod, and called 'the breastplate of judgment' because it contained the Urim and Thummim, which were used to ascertain the divine will. See Nu. xxvii. 21 and Ezr. ii. 63. Their exact form and use is not now known.

(3) Aaron bore the names of the tribes upon his shoulder (the place of strength) and upon his heart (the place of affection).

Day 7. Ex. xxix. The dedication of the priests.

It was not sufficient for Aaron and his sons simply to wear the holy garments. They must be solemnly consecrated to their office.

(1) Distinguish the various parts of the ceremony—the cleansing, the robing, the anointing, and the sacrifices.

(2) How does our High Priest stand out in marked contrast to Aaron? See Heb. vii. 26-28.

Notes.—(1) This chapter is repeated very largely in Lv. viii. The sacrifices offered may be further considered then.

(2) The word translated 'consecrate' in this chapter is different from that in xxviii. 3, which should rather be rendered 'sanctify' as in R.V. The word here means dedication to special service.

Week 27. EXODUS XXX–XXXVIII

Day 1. Ex. xxx and xxxi.

(1) (a) xxx. What two articles of furniture are here added to those already mentioned, and what is their position? (b) What does incense stand for? See Ps. cxli. 2; Rev. viii. 3, 4, v. 8 (R.V.).

What is suggested by the word 'perpetual' in verse 8? Cf. 1 Thes.
v. 17. What is the significance of verse 10? (c) At his consecration the priest's whole body was washed (Ex. xxix. 4), but there-
after, before engaging in any priestly ministry, he had to wash
his own hands and feet. What is the meaning of this for our own
service of God? See Jn. xiii. 10; 2 Cor. vii. 1; 1 Jn. i. 8, 9.

(2) xxxi. What was God's part and what man's in the design-
ing and making of the tabernacle (see verses 1-11 and cf. xxv. 2,
9)?

Day 2. Ex. xxxii.

(1) The people. How does the narrative show the strength of
the people's reaction towards idolatry? In verses 4-6 what four
acts constituted their idolatry, and which is selected for mention
by Paul in 1 Cor. x. 7?

(2) Aaron. Whom did Aaron profess still to worship? But how
did God view it? And how Moses? What was Aaron's unworthy
excuse? On whom, and on what, did he seek to throw the responsibility for his own action?

(3) Moses. What features of his character stand out in this
whole incident?

Day 3. Ex. xxxiii.

There now follows a period of suspense, during which the people mourned,
and Moses set up a tent outside the camp. Here God came in the pillar of
cloud to speak with him.

(1) Verses 1-11. What was God's attitude at this time (a) towards the people, (b) towards Moses?

(2) Verses 12-23. What were Moses' three petitions, and what
answers did God give? How does this series of petitions and
answers show on the one hand the growth of desire and faith on
Moses' part, and the richness of God's grace on the other?

Notes.—(1) Verses 1-3. The cause of mourning seems to be that God
threatens to revoke the promise of xxv. 8, xxix. 45, 46 and return to the earlier
method of guidance by His angels (see xiv. 19, xxiii. 20-23).

(2) Verse 7. This tent of meeting cannot be the tabernacle (although that
also was sometimes called by that name, see xxix. 42-44, xxxv. 21), because
it was not built yet. It was apparently an ordinary tent pitched outside the
camp during the period of suspense.

(3) Verses 14, 15. The words 'with thee' are not in the Hebrew. It would
seem that Moses understood verse 14 to mean that God would be with him
personally, and in verses 15, 16 he asks that God will go with the people also
(see xxxiv. 9). Notice the change from 'thee' in verse 14 to 'us' in verses 15, 16,
and the emphatic phrase 'I and Thy people'.

Day 4. Ex. xxxiv.

(1) Show how fully God fulfilled to Moses the promise of xxxiii. 19, and answered Moses' request. Against what, however, was Moses, as representative of the people, sternly warned?

(2) What result followed Moses' prolonged communion with God, of which others, but not himself, were conscious? What, in the case of Christians, issues from the contemplation of the glory of Christ? See 2 Cor. iii. 18; Lk. xi. 36.

Day 5. Ex. xxxv-xxxvi. 7.

(1) Note all the different kinds of person mentioned as contributing by work or gifts to the making of the tabernacle. What illustration do we find in this portion of the way in which the service of God in His Church calls for the help of all His people, whatever may be their talents, rank or age? See 1 Cor. xv. 58.

(2) What example for ourselves may be found in the spirit in which the people wrought or brought gifts, and also in the value and abundance of their giving? Cf. 2 Cor. viii. 1-5.

Day 6. Ex. xxxvi. 8-xxxvii. 9.

(1) Try to picture the holy place, as seen from within. What would the sides consist of, what the roof, what the ends, and what the floor?

(2) In Heb. x. 20 the veil is said to typify Christ's flesh. But the veil was of the same texture and appearance as the inner curtain and the curtains that formed the entrance to the holy place (see xxxvi. 8, 35, 37). Many therefore see in the holy place, as viewed thus from within, a picture of Christ as He appeared on earth: the wood of the boards representing His human nature; the gold His divine nature; the white of the fine linen representing His righteousness; the blue, His heavenly origin; the purple, His kingship; the scarlet, His sacrifice; and the floor, which was the sand of the desert, His sharing of our human lot. Ponder this picture in symbol of our Saviour.

(3) xxxvii. 1-9. How do the ark and the mercy seat also speak of Christ?

Note.—The pronoun 'he' in xxxvi. 10, 11, etc., does not represent any particular individual, but is like the French '*on*'. It might be better rendered 'they', as in Moffatt's translation. But the ark (xxxvii. 1) was Bezaleel's own work.

Day 7. Ex. xxxvii. 10-xxxviii.

(1) The tabernacle signified both God's approach to man and also man's way of drawing near to God. In the light of this fact,

what do you find signified by the table of shew-bread, the candle-stick or lamp-stand, and the altar of incense? Consider how in these symbols God offers to man communion, light, and a place for prayer, intending him to share in this communion, to receive and tend the light, and to pray continually. How are these things fulfilled to us in Christ? See Jn. vi. 57, viii. 12; Heb. iv. 16.

(2) Whence came the brass for the laver? Consider the part played by women in the making of the sanctuary. Whence came the silver for the sockets of the sanctuary? See also xxx. 11-16. What typical significance is there in the fact that the tabernacle was founded on atonement money?

Week 28. EXODUS XXXIX–LEVITICUS X

Day 1. Ex. xxxix and xl.

(1) Try to make a complete ground plan of the tabernacle, with its outer court and all its furniture in position. Then try to visualize the tabernacle, set up as here described, and the high priest and the priests in their vestments. Beautiful as it all was, what does the Epistle to the Hebrews say about it (Heb. viii. 4, 5, ix. 8-10)?

(2) What phrase occurs repeatedly in these chapters concerning the making of the tabernacle? What thoughts does this stir in our minds concerning our own service to God? Cf. Jn. v. 19, 20 and 1 Jn. ii. 6. With xl. 33b cf. Jn. xix. 30; Acts xx. 24; 2 Tim. iv. 7.

Note.—xl. 26. 'The golden altar', i.e. the altar of incense, called 'golden' to distinguish it from the brazen altar of burnt offering in the outer court (xl. 29).

Day 2. Lv. i. The burnt offering.

God is now dwelling in the midst of His people, and gives them directions concerning their worship of and communion with Him. Notice how throughout this book God is the speaker, through Moses.

(1) Verse 1. From where does God speak? See Ex. xxv. 22 and contrast Ex. xix. 3.

(2) The burnt offering. It signifies (a) that God requires entire devotion from His people (see 'burn *all*' in verses 9, 13, and of Dt. vi. 5, 6); and (b) that as the worshipper, being sinful, cannot offer such entire devotion in his own person, God has appointed a way whereby, through the death of a perfect animal ('without blemish', verse 3) offered in his stead, he may be accepted. Consider how these two features of the burnt offering, atonement (verse 4), and consecration, are fulfilled for us in Christ (see Heb. ix. 14), thereby making acceptable our own consecration of ourselves (Rom. xii. 1).

Day 3. Lv. ii and iii. The meat ('meal', R.V.) offering and the peace offering.

(1) God requires in His people, also, a blameless life (see Ps. xxiv. 3, 4; Mt. v. 48), represented by the meal offering, the *purity* of whose ingredients is emphasized (see ii. 1, 'fine flour'; ii. 11, 'no leaven'). The worshipper, unable to offer a blameless life in himself, draws near, by God's appointment, with acceptance (see ii. 2, 9, etc., 'a sweet savour') in the power of an offering possessing the perfection which he lacks. Consider how the Lord Jesus is the perfect meal-offering (Heb. vii. 26), and how in union with Him we also are called to walk after His example (1 Jn. ii. 6). With ii. 10 cf. Jn. vi. 57.

Note.—The peace offering speaks of communion, based on the blood of atonement (iii. 1, 2). See further Day 5 (2).

Day 4. Lv. iv–vi. 7. The sin and trespass (or 'guilt', R.V.) offerings.

(1) The burnt, meal, and peace offerings were offered by worshippers who were living in communion with God. But what if they have committed some sin or trespass, and communion has to be *restored?* The answer is given in today's portion: see iv. 2.

(2) With regard to the sin offering, note particularly what was done with the *blood* and with the *body* of the sacrifice (iv. 6, 7 and 11, 12). How do these solemn ordinances indicate God's hatred of sin and even suggest that sin endangers the very covenant relationship itself, which must therefore be openly re-established? Reflect on what it cost the Saviour to be our sin offering. See Is. liii. 6; Heb. xiii. 12.

Note.—The sin and trespass offerings have much in common, but the sin offering had reference rather to the *person* of the offender in his guilt Godwards, whereas the trespass offering was an atonement for the offence especially in its relation manwards. Hence the sin offering differed for different classes of persons (iv. 3, 13, 22, 27); and in the trespass offering the transgressor, in addition to his offering, had also to make amends for the wrong done (v. 16, vi. 4, 5).

Day 5. Lv. vi. 8–vii. Further instruction about the offerings, with special reference to the priests.

Distinction must be made between public and private offerings. In addition to the private burnt offerings of the people, there was a daily, public burnt offering morning and evening. See Ex. xxix. 38-42. It is this daily sacrifice that is referred to in vi. 9, 12, with directions that the fire must not be allowed to go out upon the altar.

(1) Neither the sacrifice that represented the people's consecration of themselves to God, nor the fire—which was the symbol

of Jehovah's acceptance of it—must be allowed to fail, even as He Himself fails not. What lesson does that carry for us? Cf. Heb. vi. 11, 12.

(2) vii. 11-21. In the peace offering the people offered to God the spontaneous gifts of their love. What, according to vii. 15, 16, were the three kinds of private peace offerings which individuals might bring? And what corresponding offerings are we encouraged to bring to God in Heb. xiii. 15, based, as always, on the ground of atoning blood ('*By Him* let us offer')? What corresponds in our Christian experience to the eating by the worshipper of part of the sacrifice? Cf. Ps. xxii. 26; Jn. vi. 56. With vii. 20, 21 cf. 1 Cor. xi. 27, 28.

Note.—A 'wave offering' (vii. 30) means an offering or part of an offering presented to the Lord by waving it towards Him, before receiving it back from Him. In a 'heave offering' (vii. 32) the word 'heave' does not mean to throw, but to lift or take off, and indicates the part of the offering taken off for the priests.

Day 6. Lv. viii. Dedication of the priests and tabernacle.

See Ex. xxix. 44. The directions for the ceremony were given in Ex. xxviii, xxix; this chapter gives the account of it.

(1) After the washing and the robing and the anointing came the sacrifices. Note what these latter consisted of. The anointing oil typifies the Holy Spirit. Cf. 2 Cor. i. 21; Lk. iv. 18.

(2) In the sacrifice of the ram of consecration (i.e. of dedication to special service), what special use was made of the blood? And what does this symbolism signify regarding those who are thus set apart for the service of God? What do ear, hand, and foot represent? Cf. Rom. vi. 13.

Day 7. Lv. ix and x. Aaron's entry upon his office, and the sin of his sons.

The tabernacle and priests having been sanctified and dedicated, all was now ready for the normal work of the priesthood to begin.

(1) What was Aaron's first offering in beginning his ministry? Though pardoned, anointed, and consecrated, he still needed mercy through atoning blood. But when all was duly offered, how did the Lord show in full measure His acceptance of His people's worship? With ix. 22a cf. Nu. vi. 22-27.

(2) In all the seven days of the ceremonies of dedication no incense had been offered. Whether on this account or for some other cause, what did Nadab and Abihu do? And what happened? Consider some reasons why God acted thus, and the error, or errors, against which the incident is a warning.

Notes.—(1) x. 1. 'Strange fire'. This may mean fire not taken from the altar, but the central thought is that it was fire which God had not authorized.

(2) x. 8-11. It has long been thought that Nadab and Abihu may have been indulging in wine—hence this prohibition.

(3) The significance of chapter x. 16-20 seems to be that Aaron realized that Nadab and Abihu had taken part in the offering of the sin-offering and that this rendered it unacceptable and unclean. This is a touching story of Aaron's full acceptance of God's verdict upon his own sons.

Week 29. LEVITICUS XI–XVIII

Day 1. Lv. xi. Distinction between clean and unclean.

(1) Divide the animals mentioned into the four categories of verse 46.

(2) What would these distinctions teach Israel regarding God and His worship? See verses 44, 45. Reflect also what great changes in their habits the coming of God to dwell among them brought about. Cf. 1 Pet. i. 14-16; Eph. iv. 22-24.

(3) How did our Lord show that these distinctions are not now binding? What constitutes defilement in God's sight? See Mk. vii. 14-23 (R.V.).

Day 2. Lv. xii–xiii. 46. Born unclean (xii); the plague of sin (xiii).

(1) Did the mere fact of being born a Jew give a child a place in the covenant? See verse 3 and note (1) below. How does this illustrate such passages as Ps. li. 5; Eph. ii. 3b; Jn. iii. 5?

(2) How does chapter xiii show, under the figure of leprosy, that sin is not merely acts of transgression, but something evil in men's *nature*? What parallels can you trace between the plague of sin and leprosy? Consider, for example, how marks that were outwardly small gave evidence of inward corruption. Cf. Je. xvii. 9.

Notes.—(1) Circumcision had a twofold significance, namely, identification with God's covenant people and purification from unfitness to be such.

(2) xii. 8. See Lk. ii. 22.

(3) xiii. 2. 'A bright spot'. It is said that the bright spot is often so small that it is like pustules made by the pricking of a pin.

Day 3. Lv. xiii. 47–xiv. 32.

(1) If leprosy be regarded as a type of sin, what is the general lesson enforced in xiii. 47-59 regarding sin-contaminated habits and practices? Cf. Jude 23; Rev. iii. 4.

(2) What is the significance of the fact that the leper had to be healed before he was cleansed from the defilement of his leprosy? Can a man who is not saved be sanctified?

(3) Read xiv. 4-7 in the light of Rom. vi. 3-7. Observe how washing, robing, sacrifices, consecration to God, and anointing were all required before the leper was restored to the full privilege of drawing near to God. How are all these provided for us in Christ?

Day 4. Lv. xiv. 33–xv.

(1) How does this portion show that sin, wherever found and in whatever form, is defiling in God's sight, and prevents acceptance before Him?

(2) Chapter xv is usually taken to represent the defilement of secret sin. Observe how it pollutes the whole life and all around and how this kind of defilement needs the blood of atonement no less than other forms of sin. Cf. Ps. li. 6; Mt. i. 21.

Day 5. Lv. xvi. The day of atonement.

(1) Sketch out the order of the ceremony.

(2) In what respects was the ritual of the day of atonement different from that of any other sacrifices?

(3) What do you learn from this chapter (a) regarding the conditions of approach into God's presence; (b) the defilement and need of cleansing even of the tabernacle itself; (c) the complete removal of sin's guilt through substitution; (d) the necessity on man's part of submission in penitence and faith to God's way of salvation?

Day 6. Lv. xvii.

There are two main instructions in this portion: first, that all domestic animals which are killed shall be brought to the tabernacle (verses 3-9); and second, that no blood must be eaten (verses 10-16). The former of these instructions points to a time when animals were not killed except in connection with worship of some kind.

(1) What would this first instruction (verse 3-9) teach the Israelites about God? See Dt. vi. 4. Where do you find in these verses that this instruction is directed against idolatrous worship?

(2) Why was the eating of blood so strictly forbidden? See verse 11, R.V. What clear proof is given in this verse that the idea of substitution of one life for another underlies these Old Testament sacrifices?

Day 7. Lv. xviii.

In xviii-xx the Lord passes from the worship to the *walk* of His people. Chapter xviii prohibits unlawful marriage, unchastity, and Moloch worship, but the last is dealt with more fully in xx. 2-5.

(1) What reasons are given for Israel's obedience to these laws? See verses 1-5 and 24-30. Cf. Eph. iv. 17.

(2) What application does the apostle Paul make of verse 5 in Rom. x. 5-10 and Gal. iii. 11-14? If, in Christ, 'life' is obtained through faith, are we thereby excused from obedience?

(3) What light is thrown by this chapter upon God's command for the extermination of the Canaanites?

Week 30. LEVITICUS XIX–XXVII

Day 1. Lv. xix and xx.

Chapter xix lays down a number of miscellaneous precepts relating to a holy walk. Chapter xx deals with the subject of chapter xviii.

(1) What is the special attribute of God that receives emphasis in these chapters as a ground of obedience to His commands? Cf. 1 Pet. i. 14-17.

(2) Notice how many of the commands of chapter xix centre on the thought of love to one's neighbour (verse 18b; cf. Mk. xii. 31).

(3) Why was God's anger so kindled against those who worshipped Moloch or had sympathy with such worship? See Ex. xx. 3; Je. xliv. 3, 4; Jas. iv. 4, 5 (R.V.).

Note.—Moloch was the national god of Ammon, and worship of him seems to have been associated with great cruelty. Children were offered in sacrifice and burned with fire.

Day 2. Lv. xxi and xxii. Laws concerning priests and offerings.

(1) How many separate sections do you find in these regulations?

(2) What words and expressions occur repeatedly, giving the reason why these instructions are imposed?

(3) How may we learn from this portion that things which are apparently small in themselves but which are spiritually unclean may mar our Christian life? See 2 Tim. ii. 20-22.

Day 3. Lv. xxiii. The public feasts or holy convocations of Israel.

These, as outlined in this chapter, were seven in number, including the weekly sabbath.

(1) Make a list of the feasts and note what was the general character of each. What did they have in common and what were their differences?

(2) Consider the typical significance of the three main feasts: (a) the passover (see 1 Cor. v. 7, 8); (b) the feast of weeks or pentecost (see Acts ii. 1-4); (c) the feast of tabernacles, the final ingathering of the harvest (see Rev. vii. 9). If we know the fulfil-

ment of the passover in redemption, and of pentecost in the indwelling of the Spirit, ought we not also to be looking forward to the fulfilment of the feast of tabernacles when the Lord comes again?

Notes.—(1) Verse 11. The sheaf of the first fruits of the barley harvest waved on the morrow after the sabbath points to Christ's resurrection. Cf. 1 Cor. xv. 23.

(2) Verses 16, 17. 'Fifty days'—hence the name pentecost.

(3) 'Two wave loaves'—the first fruits of the wheat harvest, representing the church of Christ in its first beginnings (Jn. xii. 24).

Day 4. Lv. xxiv.

(1) What may we learn from the word 'pure' found four times in verses 1-9? (In the Hebrew there are two words used twice each, but the meaning is similar.) Also, what may we learn from the word 'continually', also used four times? Apply these words to your own worship and service in Christ.

(2) 'Behold the goodness and the severity of God' in this chapter. Cf. Heb. x. 19-31, where the same attributes of God are set forth side by side.

Day 5. Lv. xxv.

(1) How was the year of jubilee reckoned, and what was its general purpose? Cf. Gal. v. 1.

(2) What principles are set forth in verses 17, 23, 36, 38, 42, 55 which throw light upon our own relationship to God and to one another in Christ? Cf. 1 Cor. vi. 19b, 20; Rom. vi. 14.

Day 6. Lv. xxvi.

(1) What spiritual blessings, corresponding to those promised here to an obedient Israel, are promised us in Christ? See 1 Tim. i. 14; Jn. xiv. 27; Rom. viii. 35-39; 2 Cor. vi. 16-18.

(2) The punishments fall into five groups: (a) punishments upon their persons; (b) punishments upon their possessions; (c) upon children and cattle; (d) the sword, pestilence, and famine; (e) the overthrow and exile of the nation. To what extent have they fallen upon the Jewish nation?

(3) What conditions of restoration are mentioned in verses 40-46? Cf. Dn. ix. 3-19; 2 Ch. vii. 14.

Day 7. Lv. xxvii.

Instruction as to what is to be done where an offering has been made to the Lord and the giver wants to redeem it; and also a regulation about tithes.

(1) What different cases are dealt with in this chapter?

(2) What does the chapter show of the Lord's character?

THE EPISTLE TO THE HEBREWS

INTRODUCTION

(See New Bible Handbook, pp. 389-393)

THE Epistle is an exhortation and warning to Jewish believers to continue in the faith of Christ and not to fall back into Judaism. Christ is set forth as the fulfilment of Old Testament type and prophecy, and the faith and endurance of the Old Testament saints are held up as examples to believers. Needless to say, the teaching of the Epistle has a scope and value far beyond what is of immediate concern to Jewish believers of the first century. It shows the new covenant, of which Jesus, the Son of God, is Mediator, to be not only far superior to the first covenant, but the final and perfect religion, both as regards revelation (i. 1–ii. 18) and redemption (iii. 1–x. 18). The Epistle contains also practical teaching concerning life under the new covenant. It constitutes a divine call to all who have professed themselves Christians to see that their faith is a reality, and to continue in it. It does not omit a very definite gospel message to the unsaved. It sets forth Christ very fully in His capacity as our High Priest, magnifies His divine nature, and yet points out the reality of His humility and suffering as no other book does in the whole Bible, the Gospels not excepted.

AUTHORSHIP

The Epistle is anonymous. The preponderating opinion till recently was that it was the work of the apostle Paul, but this was by no means universally held. Guesses had been made at authorship, the names of Apollos and of Priscilla, wife of Aquila, having been brought up in this connection. We need not doubt that the Epistle is Pauline in the sense that, if not written by the apostle himself, it was written by one who was familiar with, and influenced by, his teaching. The expression 'they of Italy salute you' (xiii. 24) provides a clue to the destination of the Epistle. The literal meaning is 'from Italy', and the expression suggests that the Epistle was written to a congregation of Jewish believers in Italy, and possibly in Rome.

ANALYSIS

i–ii. 18. Christ the perfect Revealer, better than angels (a) as the Son of God (i. 5-14); and (b) as the Son of Man (ii. 5-15).

iii–x. 18. Christ the perfect Redeemer, better than Moses
(iii. 1-6) and better than Aaron (a) in His person
and character (iv. 14-v. 10); (b) in the 'order'
of His priesthood (vii. 1-25); and (c) in His
ministry (viii. 1–ix. 12) and in His offering (ix.
13–x. 18).

x. 19–xii. 29. Practical teaching.

xiii. 1-25. Final counsels and greetings.

Within this outline are contained five passages of solemn warning:

ii. 1-4. Against the danger of drifting.

iii. 7–iv. 13. Against the danger of missing God's promised rest.

v. 11–vi. 20. Against the danger of losing salvation.

x. 26-39. Against the danger of drawing back.

xii. 25-29. Against the danger of refusing to hear God's final
word.

Week 31. Hebrews i–vi

Day 1. Heb. i.

(1) What seven statements are made about Christ in verses 2b
and 3? And how do these show the salvation which is through
Him to be better than all that went before?

(2) How do the Scriptures, quoted in verses 5-14, confirm the
statement of verse 4? Show how differently God speaks of Christ,
as compared with what He says of angels.

Notes.—(1) The emphasis laid upon Christ's superiority to angels, which to
us seems obvious, is explained by the fact that, to the Jews, one of the chief
glories of the Old Testament revelation was that it was given through angels.

(2) Verse 7. Angels are created beings; they are God's servants; and their
form and appearance suffer change and transformation at God's pleasure.
Contrast the royal dominion and unchanging being of the Son (verses 8-12).

Day 2. Heb. ii.

(1) Verses 1-4. What is the argument used in this warning,
and against what danger is it directed? Verse 1 should be read
in r.v.

(2) Verses 5-10. What, according to the Scriptures, is man's
destiny? And how do we see God's purpose for man being fulfilled
in Christ?

(3) Verses 11-18. In what respects is Christ *one* with us, and
because of this, what three things is He able to do for us?

Note.—In this profound passage the writer is answering an implied objection,
namely, 'Granted that the *heavenly* Christ is better than the angels, what of
Christ in the lowliness and suffering of His human life?' Cf. 1 Cor. i. 23. To

this the answer here given is threefold: (a) in God's purpose man is superior to angels; (b) under the old dispensation, while God and man drew nearer to each other, the two remained essentially separate (cf. Heb. ix. 8), but in Christ they become one; (c) hence Christ is able to redeem man and lift him up to glory, through His cross and resurrection.

Day 3. Heb. iii. 1-6.

Verse 1 is introductory to this whole section (iii. 1-x. 18); see *Analysis*. The background of the writer's thought is the redemption of Israel from Egypt and their journey to the promised land.

(1) Israel had an apostle, Moses (see note below), and a high priest, Aaron. How, in this respect, does the new covenant differ from the old? Consider the significance of the words 'holy', 'brethren', 'heavenly calling' in their practical application to our lives.

(2) Verses 2-6. See Nu. xii. 7. Can you find three points in these verses in which Christ excels Moses?

Notes.—(1) Verse 1. 'Apostle'—used here as meaning one sent upon a special mission. Cf. Ex. iii. 10; Jn. xx. 21.

(2) Verse 2. 'His house', that is, the people of God, in the midst of whom God dwells as in a house or household.

(3) Verse 6. The word 'hope' is one of the important words of the Epistle, expressing the glorious future to be ushered in at the second coming of Christ. See vi. 11, 18, vii. 19, x. 23 (R.V.).

Day 4. Heb. iii. 7–iv. 13.

The R.V. should be used throughout this portion.

(1) What passage of Scripture is expounded in iii. 7-19, and what warning do we receive from it? Observe specially the description of the danger given in verses 12 and 13 and how it may be averted; also *who it was* that sinned and perished in this way. See verses 16-19, R.V.

(2) By what argument is it shown in iv. 3-9 that the rest of God ('My rest'), which Israel lost by unbelief, remains still to be possessed? How is it defined, and what is the condition of obtaining it? See verses 1, 2, and 9.

(3) What fivefold description is given in iv. 12 of God's word, one portion of which the writer has just been expounding? How should these characteristics of God's word, together with the fact that He knows all our heart (iv. 13), stir us to diligence (iv. 11)?

Day 5. Heb. iv. 14–v. 10. Jesus the perfect High Priest in His person and character.

The writer has now reached the beginning of the central and most important part of the Epistle (see *Analysis*), in which he shows that the Christian faith, as a religion of redemption, is the final religion, having achieved *eternal* redemption (ix. 12).

(1) iv. 14-16. What two things are we told to do, and on what grounds?

(2) v. 1-10. What characteristics of a true priest are set forth in verses 1-4 concerning (a) his function; (b) his disposition; and (c) his appointment to office? And how do verses 5-10 show that, in Jesus, these characteristics are found in perfection? See Note (2) below.

Notes.—(1) 'Profession' or 'confession' (R.V.), another important word in this Epistle. The open confession of our faith is throughout insisted upon (see x. 23, xi. 13, xiii. 13).

(2) In verses 5-10 the writer reverses the order of treatment, taking first, appointment to office (verses 5, 6); second, disposition (verses 7, 8); and third, function (verses 9, 10).

(3) Verses 7-10 give us a very sacred and very amazing insight into the earthly humility and human nature of our Lord.

Day 6. Heb. v. 11-vi. 8.

As the writer is about to begin his exposition of the Melchisedec priesthood of Christ, he is arrested by a sense of the difficulty of expounding it to people, the ears of whose minds have become dulled.

(1) v. 11-14. What is the writer's complaint about his readers? How is it with ourselves? Have we been growing in spiritual knowledge or are we still feeding upon elementary Christian teaching?

(2) vi. 1-3. What teaching constitutes the foundation of the gospel? See Acts ii. 38, viii. 37, xvii. 31, xix. 3-6, xx. 21, xxiv. 25.

(3) vi. 4-8. What reason is given here for not laying again this foundation?

Notes.—(1) 'Perfection', that is, the perfection offered in Christ. Cf. Col. i. 28.

(2) The solemn warning in verses 4-6 (cf. x. 26-31) is a difficulty to some. It is best taken as referring to professors, who have 'tasted' and then rejected without assimilating.

Day 7. Heb. vi. 9-20.

(1) What gives the writer confidence as to his readers' final salvation (verses 9-10)? But what does he desire concerning them (verses 11, 12)?

(2) Verses 13-20. What unshakable grounds of assurance have we that, if we have made our refuge in Christ, our hope will not be put to shame? Yet what qualities does a true 'laying hold' demand? See verses 12, 15, and cf. iii. 6, x. 36; Lk. xxi. 19 (R.V.).

Week 32. Hebrews vii–x

Day 1. Heb. vii. 1-14. Christ as High Priest superior in the 'order' of His priesthood.

(1) What characteristics of Melchisedec, as he stands portrayed in Scripture (Gn. xiv. 18-20), does the writer mention in verses 1-3?

(2) On what grounds is Melchisedec shown in verses 4-10 to be superior to the Levitical priesthood?

(3) What evidence is adduced in verses 11-14 to show that the Aaronic priesthood was essentially defective and not intended to be permanent, and that this carried with it a change also in regard to *the law*?

Note.—The writer does not stay to expound all the characteristics of Melchisedec which he mentions in verses 1-3, but concentrates on those which depict him as abiding a priest in perpetuity, and thus being a type of the Son of God.

Day 2. Heb. vii. 15-28.

(1) Verses 15-19. See Ps. cx. 4 ('for ever'). What double contrast is here brought out between the Levitical and Melchisedec orders of priesthood? How does this show that the two orders are incompatible, and that the introduction of the second implies the abrogation of the first?

(2) Verses 20-22. See Ps. cx. 4 ('The Lord hath sworn'). What is the significance of God's oath? Notice particularly the words 'will not repent', and cf. vi. 17.

(3) Verses 23-28. How do these verses show that in Jesus we have a perfect High Priest, and that He perfectly meets the sinner's need?

Notes.—(1) Verse 16. 'The law of a carnal commandment', that is, a legal code moving in the sphere of physical qualifications, and therefore within the limitations of mortality. Contrast 'the power of an indissoluble life' in Christ. See R.V. mg.

(2) Verse 25. 'To the uttermost', both of time and of degree.

Day 3. Heb. viii.

The writer is now about to enter upon a new aspect of Christ's Priesthood, namely, His High Priestly ministry. In this chapter he shows that this ministry is exercised (a) in a better sanctuary, not on earth but in heaven (verses 1-5); and (b) in connection with a better covenant (verses 6-13). Cf. Je. xxxi. 31-34; Mt. xxvi. 28.

(1) Verses 1-5. Some hearts perhaps craved that Christ might be on earth, ministering in the earthly sanctuary. What twofold answer is given in these verses?

(2) Verses 6-13. What is said here about the first covenant? And what four particulars are given of the new covenant, showing its superiority? Are these things known to you in glad experience?

Day 4. Heb. ix. 1-14. Christ the High Priest of a better sanctuary.

(1) Verses 1-8. In this description of the furnishings and service of the earthly sanctuary, to what feature is attention specially drawn? And what does the Holy Spirit teach us by it?

(2) Verses 9-10. In what respect did the gifts and sacrifices of the earthly sanctuary fail of effect, and for what reason?

(3) Verses 11-14. How do the service and sacrifice of Christ, both in their essential character and in their result, stand out in contrast to the service and sacrifices of the first covenant?

Notes.—(1) Verse 4. 'The golden censer'. The Greek word may also mean 'the golden altar of incense' (see R.V. mg.). Some take the reference to be the censer used on the day of atonement (Lv. xvi. 12, 13). The altar of incense was not in the holy of holies (Ex. xl. 26).

(2) Verses 6 and 8. 'The first tabernacle' here means 'the holy place', as distinct from the holy of holies.

(3) Verse 9. 'As touching the conscience make the worshipper perfect' (R.V.), that is, free the conscience from guilt and defilement. See also verse 14.

Day 5. Heb. ix. 15-28.

Further instances are here given of the preciousness and power of the blood of Christ: first, in relation to the new covenant (verses 15-23); and second, as being a single sacrifice, offered once for all (verses 24-28).

(1) What was the one thing necessary for making a covenant?

(2) How does the fact that Christ offered one sacrifice prove its abiding efficacy? See verses 24-26.

(3) Observe the contrast in verses 27 and 28 between (a) sinful man—appointed to death—going to judgment; and (b) the Saviour—dying for our sins—returning in salvation. Are you among those who 'look for Him'?

Note.—It is best, as in R.V., to read 'covenant' throughout this passage, except in verses 16 and 17, where the meaning seems to be 'testament' or 'will'. The Greek word has both meanings.

Day 6. Heb. x. 1-18. Final exposition of Christ's sacrifice.

(1) Verses 1-4. In what three ways were the sacrifices of the tabernacle inadequate?

(2) Verses 5-10. What is the new and different sacrifice offered by Christ, and what is its efficacy (verse 10)? 'Sanctified' here means brought into a relationship of acceptance and service with God for ever.

(3) Verses 11-18. The difference between the two systems is here summed up. Write down as many contrasts as you can find. How has the abiding validity of Christ's sacrifice been attested by the Holy Ghost?

Notes.—(1) Verse 5. The writer here, as elsewhere, quotes from the Greek version of the Old Testament.

(2) Verse 14. 'Perfected' etc. The meaning is that by the one sacrifice of Christ everything that hinders our access to God is removed.

Day 7. Heb. x. 19-39.

Having finished his doctrinal exposition, the writer proceeds to give practical counsel for the life we are to live under the new covenant (see *Analysis*).

(1) Verses 19-25. What is to be (a) the believer's relation to God; (b) his witness in the world; and (c) his responsibility to his fellow believers?

(2) Verses 26-39. Consider the terrible doom of the apostate in contrast to the blessedness described in x. 19-22. What various reasons for steadfast endurance does the writer urge in verses 32-39? Cf. Gal. iii. 4.

Notes.—(1) Verse 22. As the high priest and his sons at their consecration for service in the earthly sanctuary were washed with water and sprinkled with the blood of sacrifice (Ex. xxix. 4, 21), so we in 'heart' and 'body', that is, inwardly and outwardly, in our whole being, have been made clean in Christ.

(2) Verses 22, 23 (R.V.), 24. Note the combination of faith, hope, and love, as in 1 Cor. xiii. 13; 1 Thes. i. 3.

Week 33. HEBREWS XI-XIII

Day 1. Heb. xi. 1-22. The importance of faith. See also vi. 12 and x. 38.

(1) In how many different ways is faith manifested in this portion? In what way or ways is faith manifested in your life?

(2) What changes were brought into the lives of the people here mentioned, and what results did faith effect?

(3) What is the ultimate end of those who live by faith?

Day 2. Heb. xi. 23-40.

(1) Verses 24-27. How did Moses by faith overcome (a) the allurements of the world; and (b) the threats of the world? Observe the emphasis laid in both cases upon the *vision* that faith gives. Cf. 1 Jn. v. 4; 2 Cor. iv. 18.

(2) Verses 28-31. Consider in these four instances of faith how difficult it must have been to exercise faith, and the great results that followed.

(3) Verses 32-38. A summary of the achievements (verses 32-
35a) and the sufferings (verses 35b-38) of faith. What challenge
is presented to us by the fact that these men and women lived
before Christ?

Day 3. Heb. xii. 1-17.

(1) Verses 1-4. What three conditions must be fulfilled if the
Christian race is to be run and the prize attained? Cf. 1 Cor. ix.
24-26; Phil. iii. 13, 14.

(2) Verses 5-11. How are we to look upon suffering, if it befall
us, and what is to be our attitude under it?

(3) Verses 12-17 set forth what should be our attitude towards
others in times of trial. What is said here about helping the weak,
about pursuing high aims (verse 14), and about mutual responsibility and watchful oversight? Cf. x. 24, 25; Gn. iv. 9.

Day 4. Heb. xii. 18-29.

(1) Verses 18-24. Final contrast between the two covenants.
In what respects does the heavenly Mount Zion of the new
covenant excel in glory the earthly mountain Sinai of the first
covenant? Cf. 2 Cor. iii. 7-11.

(2) Verses 25-29. What is the danger against which warning
is here given? Try to state in your own words the two main points
of the argument.

Note.—Verses 22 and 23. The central words of these two verses may be
interpreted either as applying solely to angels (the word 'church' meaning
'convocation') or as indicating two separate companies: the angels, and the
Church. The first of these alternatives is probably to be preferred. This Epistle
does not elsewhere speak of the Church as signifying the whole body of the
redeemed in Christ, nor does the writer conceive of the Church as being, at
the time he wrote, in heaven. The only human beings he sees there, as a
separate company, are the Old Testament saints, now made perfect through
Christ's sacrifice. But he does see the angels, gathered there in festal assembly,
a convocation of the firstborn of heaven's citizens. His purpose is to show that
whereas at Sinai the people saw only a temporary manifestation of angels, we,
through the new covenant, are brought into abiding fellowship with them in
their life and worship in the eternal city.

Day 5. Heb. xiii. 1-8.

(1) What various aspects of Christian duty are set forth in these
verses? What gracious promise is quoted? What should be our
response?

(2) In what two ways should Christian leaders, whose life on
earth has ended, be remembered (verse 7, R.V.)? What is the
connection between verses 7 and 8?

Note.—Verse 1. 'Continue'. Cf. vi. 10, x. 33, 34.

Day 6. Heb. xiii. 9-25.

(1) If, because of our confession of Christ, we must suffer the loss of former earthly fellowships, what two sources of comfort are here brought before us? See verses 12-14 and note below.

(2) What sacrifices has the Christian to offer?

(3) What is the difference between the two petitions of the great prayer of verses 20, 21? And on what massive foundations are they based?

Notes.—(1) Verse 9. It would appear that the readers of the Epistle were being urged to partake of sacrificial meals, such as were common under the law, to maintain fellowship with the non-Christian Jewish community. The writer reminds them (a) that grace, not food, strengthens the soul; (b) that the sacrifice of Christ was essentially a sin offering, in connection with which, under the law, there was no sacrificial meal (verses 10, 11; cf. Lv. iv. 11, 12, 20, 21); (c) if they would have fellowship, therefore, with Christ, it will not be by staying within the camp of Judaism, but by going forth to Him 'without the camp'.

(2) Verse 21. 'Make you perfect', that is, repair and equip, putting into a fit condition to serve him.

Day 7. Revision.

Consider the two covenants. (a) How was the first covenant defective in its sanctuary, its priesthood, and its sacrifices? (b) How in all these things is the second covenant perfect? Are we availing ourselves, as we should, of our privileges in Christ Jesus?

PSALMS I—XLI

INTRODUCTION

(See New Bible Handbook, pp. 186, 187, 191-198)

THE Book of Psalms may be regarded as the inspired hymn-book of the Jewish Church, containing psalms for both public and private worship. Those with the superscription (or subscription)[1] 'To the chief musician' seem specially intended for public worship. Others were, perhaps, originally personal meditations which were taken over for use in the service of the sanctuary and in family worship at home. There are also didactic poems and historical recitals. The book stood at the head of the third section of the

---

[1] A reference to Hab. iii. 19 (last clause) suggests the probability that, in those of the psalms which have headings or titles, the musical part of the title, including words 'To the Chief musician', should really be attached to the end of the precedin psalm.

Hebrew Scriptures, to which it often gave its name.[1] This section followed the books of the prophets.

The contents of the book were composed at various periods during the whole of Israelite history from the exodus to the Babylonian captivity. One psalm at least is the work of Moses (Ps. xc). Many are by David, one or two by Solomon, a few by certain of the Temple singers, and many again are anonymous. Some have a title and others have none. The psalms divide into five divisions, as follows: i–xli, xlii–lxxii, lxxiii–lxxxix, xc–cvi, cvii–cl. The end of each division except the last is marked by the word 'Amen'.

This third section of the Old Testament Scriptures, at the beginning of which the psalms stand, may be said to strike, on the whole, a more individual note than the preceding ones. While the prophets write largely (though not, of course, entirely) from the point of view of the outward and national life, the psalms deal largely with personal spiritual matters. It is needless to say that they look forward, as do the prophets, to the Person and work of our Lord Jesus Christ.

The R.V. should be used throughout the study of the psalms.

Week 34. Psalms i–xii

Day 1. Pss. i and ii.

(1) Sum up in two headings, one negative, the other positive, the characteristics of the righteous as given in Ps. i. 1, 2. Have we proved for ourselves the blessedness (as pictured in verse 3) of conforming to this standard? In the light of the gospel, who are 'the righteous'?

(2) Contrast in i. 4-6 the final end of the righteous, as compared with that of the 'ungodly' (R.V. 'wicked').

(3) What reasons are given in Ps. ii why rebellion against the Lord and His anointed king is, and must be, 'a vain thing'? Cf. Acts iv. 25-28.

Notes.—(1) i. 2. 'The law of the Lord'; i.e. the revealed will of Jehovah.

(2) i. 3. 'Planted'; better 'transplanted'. The picture is that of a tree selected by the owner of an orchard, and transplanted near to the irrigation channels by which the garden was watered.

(3) i. 6. 'Knoweth'; in the sense of 'careth for'. Cf. Na. i. 7.

(4) Ps. ii is the first of what are known as messianic psalms, that is, psalms which prophesy the sufferings and glory of the coming Messiah.

Day 2. Pss. iii and iv.

For the circumstances in which these psalms were written see 2 Sa. xv-xvii.

[1] See, e.g. Lk. xxiv. 44.

(1) Ps. iii is a morning psalm. As David wakes, what adverse conditions confront him (see verses 1, 2)? How does he strengthen his faith (verses 2-5), until it rises into confident assurance of victory (verses 6-8)? What may we learn from his example in our own conflicts?

(2) Ps. iv is an evening psalm. In verses 2-5 David addresses his adversaries. What counsel does he give them? and in what does he find his own strength, joy, and security?

Notes.—(1) iii. 5. If this psalm was written, as seems likely, on the second morning after David's flight from Jerusalem, it was a great encouragement to him that the night had passed without an attack. Cf. 2 Sa. xvii. 1, 16.

(2) iv. 3. 'Him that is godly.' A reference to David himself; see r.v. mg. and 2 Sa. v. 2; Ps. lxxviii. 70, 71.

(3) iv. 4. 'Stand in awe'; the Hebrew word literally means 'tremble', whether with fear or anger. The LXX takes it to mean 'tremble with anger' (cf. r.v. mg.) and Paul follows this in Eph. iv. 26. If it be taken as 'tremble with fear', the meaning is 'stand in awe' of God who is my avenger, and 'sin not', i.e. desist from your rebellion.

Day 3. Ps. v.

(1) What does this psalm reveal about God?

(2) Study the psalm as an example of prayer. When, how, for what, and why does David pray?

(3) Do we also pray much, hate evil, and rejoice greatly?

Day 4. Ps. vi.

Another example of prayer. Note the divisions, first an anguished cry (verses 1-3), second, calmer pleading, with reasons why God should answer (verses 4-7), third, the victory of faith (verses 8-10).

(1) Do you know in experience how thus to 'fight the good fight of faith', rising from a sense of overwhelming need to an assurance of answered prayer and certain deliverance? Cf. Ps. lxii. 8.

Note.—David seems to have suffered both from sickness and from the taunts of his enemies. His sickness gave them occasion to point to him as one 'smitten of God'.

Day 5. Pss. vii and viii.

(1) Ps. vii falls into two parts. The first part (verses 1-10) consists of an impassioned protestation of innocence in the face of ruthless persecution, and an appeal to God for judgment. On what grounds is David's confidence based?

(2) The second part of the psalm (verses 11-17) consists of reflections on the certain doom of the wicked, followed by an ascription of praise to God. In what two ways does judgment

overtake the wicked? See verses 11-13 and 14-16, and compare
Ps. xxxiv. 16; Pr. xxvi. 26, 27.

(3) What light is thrown upon Ps. viii (a) by our Lord's reference to it in Mt. xxi. 16, and (b) by Heb. ii. 5-9?

Notes.—(1) Ps. vii probably belongs to the period in David's life when he
was being hunted by Saul. It is not known who Cush was, except that he was
a man of Saul's tribe.

(2) vii. 7. The word 'return' is difficult to explain. It is possible that the
word should be rendered 'sit'. Verses 6-9 are a picture of God seated in judgment.

Day 6. Pss. ix and x.

These psalms were probably originally one, as is shown by the fact of their
common 'alphabetic' structure. In the LXX they are one psalm. The contents
are, however, different. Ps. ix is mainly a song of praise, celebrating victory
over foreign nations; but Ps. x consists mainly of prayer, pleading for the overthrow of the wicked within Israel.

(1) What does David say about the Lord, especially in Ps. ix?
To how much of what he says can you say 'Amen' from your own
experience?

(2) What is said in these two psalms, and especially in Ps. x,
about the wicked man—his thoughts, his actions, and his final
end?

Notes.—(1) ix. 8. 'People'; better, 'peoples' (R.V.), and so also in verse 11.
The whole psalm has to do with God's judgment upon the surrounding nations.

(2) ix. 17. 'Hell'; not the place of torment, but 'Sheol' (R.V.), the place of
the dead. The meaning is that through the judgments which God is executing,
the life of the wicked will be cut short by death.

Day 7. Pss. xi and xii.

(1) Why did not David follow the counsel given him to flee in
the hour of peril? What vision did he see that gave him confidence? Cf. Ne. vi. 10-13; Heb. xi. 27. But is it always wrong
to flee in face of danger? Cf. Jn. x. 39, 40; Acts ix. 24-26; Mt. x.
23.

(2) How are the word of man and the Word of God contrasted
in Ps. xii?

Notes.—(1) xi. 3. Better, perhaps, as in R.V. mg. The righteous have not
been able to effect any change for the better; why then remain in the midst of
danger?

(2) xii. 3 may be rendered as a prayer. 'May the Lord cut off', etc.

(3) xii. 5. God's answer to the prayer.

Week 35. PSALMS XIII–XXI

Day 1. Pss. xiii and xiv.

(1) Notice the delay in the answer to David's prayer. How did
he act in the face of it? Cf. Lk. xviii. 1.

(2) Have we known what it is thus to experience delay in receiving an answer from God, until circumstances became, humanly speaking, almost desperate (xiii. 3, 4); and yet, like David, to rise through faith to a triumphant assurance of coming blessing? Cf. Mk. xi. 24 (R.V.).

(3) What do we learn from Ps. xiv about the extent of the corruption that has befallen man, and about the reason for it?

Notes.—(1) Ps. xiv is most probably a national psalm. Verses 1-3 refer to mankind in general and verses 4-6 to some cruel oppression of Israel, such as that of Pharaoh, and God's deliverance of His people.

(2) xiv. 5. 'There were they in great fear'; a reference perhaps to the destruction of the Egyptians (Ex. xiv. 30).

(3) xiv. 7. 'Bringeth back the captivity'; better, perhaps, 'restores the ortunes of'. It is not necessarily an allusion to the Exile, for the same phrase used by the pre-exilic prophets, see Ho. vi. 11; Am. ix. 14.

Day 2. Pss. xv and xvi.

(1) As you read Ps. xv are you not impressed by two facts, (1) that clause by clause the Psalmist's description is fulfilled in Christ, and (2) that clause by clause, *we* have come short? What has the gospel to say to us in this situation? See Heb. x. 19-22, xiii. 20, 21; Jude 24, 25.

(2) What, according to Ps. xvi, are the marks of the believing man (verses 1-4), what his privileges (verses 5-8), and what his prospects (verses 9-11)?

Notes.—(1) xv. 5a. See Lv. xxv. 35-37. 'The positive rule of the Old Testament has become obsolete under the circumstances of modern society, but the principle which underlies it is still of obligation' (*Camb. Bible*).

(2) xvi. 2 and 3. It is important here to follow the R.V. (as also in verses 4, 9, 10). Note also the distinction between LORD (Jehovah) and Lord (sovereign Master).

(3) xvi. 7. 'My reins'; literally 'kidneys', used figuratively as representing the inward feelings.

(4) xvi. 10. Quoted by Peter (Acts ii. 27) and by Paul (Acts xiii. 35) with reference to Christ. As with Ps. xv, the psalm is fulfilled in Him, and in us through Him.

Day 3. Ps. xvii.

The background of the psalm is a situation of extreme peril (verses 9, 11) arising from the attacks of evil men. The R.V. is of special value here.

(1) In verses 1-7 on what two grounds does David base his plea? Cf. Jn. xvi. 27; 1 Jn. iii. 21, 22.

(2) How are his enemies described (a) in their inward character, (b) in their attitude towards the Psalmist, (c) in their aims and outlook?

(3) What kept David from being corrupted by his evil environment, and what contrast is set forth between his own desires and those of his enemies? Are we like him in this?

Notes.—(1) Verse 4. 'The ways of the violent'; cf. xxxiv. 10, lxii. 10.
(2) Verse 9. 'My deadly enemies'; i.e. enemies who seek my death.
(3) Verse 10a. See R.V. mg. and cf. 1 Jn. iii. 17.

Day 4. Ps. xviii. 1-27.

This great psalm must be read in the light of David's life-story as described in 1 Sa. xvi-2 Sa. viii. King of a united nation, victorious over surrounding peoples, blessed with the great promise of the continuance of his royal line, David magnifies the power and goodness of his God.

(1) Verses 1-3. Cliff, fortress, rock, shield—these had been David's places of refuge; but God, he says, was more to him than them all. What are the defences and securities in which men trust today? Is God to you all that these can give, and more? Cf. Hab. iii. 17, 18; Phil. iv. 12, 13.

(2) Verses 12-19. To what does David bear testimony in these verses and how do they encourage us to bring our own need to God, however dark the outlook? Cf. Ps. lxii. 8.

(3) Verses 20-27. David declares that his deliverance is a reward for his righteousness, and that God's dealings with men are according to their moral character. Is this the case and, if so, what hope is there for sinners?

Note.—Verses 9-16 are probably not intended to be taken literally, but as a poetic description in vivid imagery of the strength and majesty with which God came to David's aid. There is no record of God's scattering David's enemies by an actual storm.

Day 5. Ps. xviii. 28-50.

(1) Make a list of all that God did for David, as set forth in these verses. What corresponding help may we expect from Him in spiritual service? Cf. 1 Cor. xv. 10; Eph. i. 19.

(2) According to Rom. xv. 9 (where verse 49 of the psalm is applied to Christ) the psalm may be regarded as a prophetic anticipation of the final triumph of Christ over all His enemies and of His universal reign. Have you ever pondered this glorious consummation and given thanks?

Notes.—(1) Verse 29. 'Through a troop'; better, 'after a troop'; a probable allusion to 1 Sa. xxx. 8. The next clause may allude to 2 Sa. v. 6, 7.
(2) Verse 35. 'Gentleness' or 'condescension' (R.V. mg.). Literally 'humbleness of mind'. Cf. Ps. cxiii. 5-8; Is. lvii. 15; Mt. xi. 29; Phil. ii. 5-8.

Day 6. Ps. xix.

(1) Describe in your own words what the heavens, the firmament, day and night, the sun, tell us of God (verses 1-6). Cf. Jb. xxxviii. 31-35; Pss. lxxiv. 16, cxlviii. 3-6; Mt. v. 45.

(2) Contrast with this the revelation given in the law (verses 7-11) showing how great is the advance, both in clearness, and fulness of effect.

(3) Do we share the Psalmist's deep desire for deliverance from sin, and for acceptance with God? How does the gospel provide a better solution for the problem of sin? See Note (2) below, also Acts xiii. 38, 39; Rom. viii. 1-4.

Notes.—(1) Verse 4. 'Their line'; i.e. their 'measuring line'. Cf. Je. xxxi. 39. The boundary of their message is earth's farthest limit.

(2) Verses 11-13. The law provided an atonement for sins of ignorance (here called 'hidden faults'), but not for deliberate wilful sinning (here called 'presumptuous sins'). See Lv. iv. 2; Nu. xv. 30, 31. Therefore the Psalmist prays that he may not be held guilty for the former (it being assumed that the sacrifices have been offered), and that he may be withheld from the latter.

Day 7. Pss. xx and xxi.

These two psalms are closely linked together. In Ps. xx a battle is about to take place between the king of Israel at the head of his people, and his foes. Sacrifices have been offered, and the king with his people commit their cause in faith to God. In Ps. xxi the battle is won, and the people give thanks to God for their king, and look forward to further victories.

(1) Ps. xx falls into two parts, verses 1-5 and 6-8, with a concluding prayer. What is the keynote of the first part, and what of the second? Observe the threefold mention of the Name of God.

(2) Ps. xxi also falls into two parts, verses 1-7 and 8-12, with a concluding prayer. To whom is the first part addressed, and to whom the second? Show how what is said of the king finds its fulfilment in Christ.

(3) What is the secret of the king's joy? Do we know the same secret? Cf. Ne. viii. 10 (last clause).

Week 36. PSALMS XXII–XXIX

Day 1. Ps. xxii. 1-21.

This is a prophetic psalm 'testifying beforehand the sufferings of Christ, and the glory that should follow' (1 Pet. i. 11). It falls into four sections or strophes, of which today we study the first three.

(1) Verses 1-10. In this strophe faith wrestles to hold fast to the fact that Jehovah is '*my* God', and wins the victory. What did the sufferer's enemies say, and on what, in face of these taunts, did his faith stay itself? With verses 6-8 cf. Mt. xxvii. 39-43, and with verse 1 cf. Mt. xxvii. 46.

(2) Verses 11-18. The sufferer pours out his heart before the Lord. Consider what an exact picture is given here of the Passion scenes in the Gospels. With verse 18, for example, cf. Mt. xxvii. 35; Jn. xix. 23, 24.

(3) Verses 19-21. Faith wins the victory. This third strophe is cut short by the shout of assurance that God has heard and answered. See Note (4) below.

Notes.—(1) Verse 3. 'Inhabitest'; better, 'art enthroned upon' as in R.V. mg.—a beautiful picture of the praises of Israel rising as a cloud to form a throne, on which God sits.

(2) Verse 14. 'Wax', 'melted'; a symbol of faintness. See Jos. ii. 11.

(3) Verse 20. 'My darling'; literally 'my only one', that is, 'my one precious life'.

(4) Verse 21. This verse might be written thus:

'Save me from the lion's mouth
From the wild oxen's horns. . .
Thou hast answered me.'

Contrast this with verse 2, 'Thou answerest not'.

Day 2. Ps. xxii. 22-31.

In this fourth strophe of the psalm we are in a different world, a world of praise, worship, and vision of divine triumph.

(1) Trace in these verses some of the happy results of the sufferings described in verses 1-21.

(2) This closing strophe might have been thought exaggerated before Jesus came. How could the deliverance of one sufferer be the cause of all nations and classes worshipping the Lord, and be the theme of unending story from generation to generation? Yet in the light of the New Testament, how is the prophecy seen not only to have been fulfilled, but far exceeded?

Notes.—(1) Verse 22. This is applied to Christ in Heb. ii. 12.

(2) Verse 25. 'I will pay my vows'; i.e. by sacrifice. Cf. Pss. lxvi. 13, cxvi. 17, 18. At such sacrifices others gathered round, and shared in the feast (Dt. xii. 18, xvi. 11, 14). The Psalmist sees a great company gathered—'the meek', 'all the ends of the earth', 'rich and poor', 'from generation to generation'.

Day 3. Pss. xxiii and xxiv.

(1) How does Ps. xxiii show that he who trusts in the Lord lacks for nothing? In other words, what good things did David find under the care of his Shepherd? Make a list of them, verse by verse.

(2) What may be learned about the King of glory from verses 1 and 2 of Ps. xxiv, and what from verses 3-5? What is required of His worshippers in hand, heart, soul, and lips?

Note.—Ps. xxiv. There is little doubt that this psalm was composed to be sung when David brought the ark of God to Jerusalem (see 2 Sa. vi). In the worship of the Christian Church, verses 7-10 have been interpreted of Christ's ascension. They are rather a prophecy of the return of the Lord Jesus as the King of glory to set up His kingdom on Mount Zion. Cf. Is. xxiv. 23.

Day 4. Ps. xxv.

This is one of the so-called alphabetic psalms. In the Hebrew text each two lines (with one or two exceptions) begin with a fresh letter of the Hebrew alphabet, in order. The Psalm begins and ends with a series of petitions (verses 1-7 and 15-21), and in the centre is a section consisting of reflections on the character and ways of God (verses 8-14). Verse 22 seems to have been added later.

(1) What three main petitions does the Psalmist make in verses 1-7, and what in verses 15-21? What light do the petitions throw upon his circumstances and spiritual experience? Are the last two lines of verse 5 true of you also?

(2) What in verses 8-14 is said about God, and what He does for those who fear Him? Do you believe these things; and if so, what effect should they have upon your life?

Day 5. Ps. xxvi.

The psalm centres in the prayer of verse 9, where David prays that he may not share the fate of the wicked. Often in his early life must it have seemed that he was about to be cut off.

(1) On what grounds in verses 1-8 does he base his plea?

(2) Describe in your own words the main trend of David's life as he describes it here? Can you make a similar claim for yourself?

(3) How does the closing verse show that David has reached the assurance that his prayer is answered? Compare Week 34, Day 4 (1).

Notes.—(1) Verse 2. 'Examine . . . prove . . . try'; a searching test both of outward conduct and of inward thought.

(2) Verse 6. Cf. xxiv. 3, 4; Ex. xxx. 19, 20.

(3) Verse 8. 'Thine honour'; better, as in R.V., 'Thy glory'. Cf. Ex. xl. 34.

(4) Verse 12. 'An even place'; i.e. a place of safety and ease, where he can fulfil the promises of verses 6 and 7.

Day 6. Ps. xxvii.

The psalm falls into two parts, which are very different in character. In the first part David's heart is full of confidence and praise (verses 1-6); in the second his spirit is oppressed, and he pleads anxiously for help (verses 7-14).

(1) Does Christian experience also know such variations of

mood? Cf., e.g., Lk. x. 17-24 with xxii. 39-46, and Rom. viii. 35-39
with 2 Cor. vii. 5, 6.

(2) In verses 1-6 what does David say the Lord is to him, and
will do for him, and what is David's chief desire? Cf. Ps. xci. 1, 2.

(3) In verses 7-14 what are David's seven petitions? How does
he address God, and how does he encourage himself to continue
in prayer? Cf. 1 Sa. xxx. 6 (last clause).

Note.—Verse 10. The first clause is probably a proverbial expression
indicating great need, such as that of a deserted child.

Day 7. Pss. xxviii and xxix.

(1) Many have thought that the circumstances portrayed in
Ps. xxviii correspond to David's situation at the time of his flight
from Absalom. What points of correspondence can you discern?

(2) On what attributes of God does David rely in presenting his
petition? How rich and full also his thanksgiving for God's
answer to his cry! Can you say verse 7 as the witness and resolve
of your own heart?

(3) Ps. xxix is the description of a thunderstorm viewed as a
manifestation of God's glory. What spiritual lessons does it teach
regarding God and regarding our duties and privileges as His
people? Notice how verses 1 and 11 are combined in the angels'
song in Lk. ii. 14.

Notes.—(1) xxix. 3. 'The voice of the Lord'; i.e. thunder, and so throughout
the psalm. Cf. xviii. 13.

(2) Verse 6. 'Sirion'; an old name for Hermon. See Dt. iii. 9.

(3) Verse 7. 'Divideth (or 'cleaveth', R.V.) the flames of fire'. A reference
to flashes of lightning.

(4) Verses 9 and 10 should be read as in the R.V.

Week 37. PSALMS XXX–XXXVI
Day 1. Ps. xxx.

(1) From what danger had God delivered David, and what
indications are there that the danger had been very great? This
gave rise to reflections in his mind, first, about sorrow in general,
and second, about his own life. What does he say about sorrow
(verse 5)?

(2) In regard to his own life, to what conclusions does David
come as to (a) the salutary effects of the affliction, (b) the purpose
for which he had been delivered?

Notes.—(1) Verse 3. See R.V. mg. David was already, as it were, among the
dead.

(2) Verse 5. See R.V. It is a beautiful picture. Weeping, like a passing traveller, lodges for the night only: the morning light brings Joy to abide. Cf. verse 11.

(3) Verse 12. 'My glory'; i.e., my soul.

Day 2. Ps. xxxi.

In this psalm David, beginning with an urgent sense of need, and rising by the exercise of faith to the heights of praise (verses 1-8), is suddenly cast down to deeper depths than before, and has to fight the fight of faith anew (verses 9-18) until at last he stands triumphantly upon the uplands of song (verses 19-24).

(1) Notice in verse 2 the words 'Be Thou', and in verse 3 'Thou art'. 'It is the logic', says Delitzsch, 'of every believing prayer'. In prayer do you stop at 'Be Thou', or go on to say by faith 'Thou art'?

(2) What would you pick out as the most bitter ingredient in David's cup of sorrow (verses 9-18)? What would you do if you were in like case? What did David do?

(3) In verses 19-24 what witness does David bear to God, and what message does he bring to fellow-believers everywhere? If we accept and act on the message, what will follow? Shall not we also prove the witness true, and thus be able to encourage others?

Notes.—(1) Verse 5a. See Lk. xxiii. 46, an evidence that this psalm was in our Lord's mind upon the cross.

(2) Verse 8. 'In a large place' (R.V.); with liberty of movement, in contrast to being 'shut up' (verse 8a).

(3) Verse 10. 'Iniquity'; the LXX reads here 'affliction'.

(4) Verse 12. Is this a reference to David's time of exile? Cf. 1 Sa. xxvi. 19.

(5) Verse 23c. 'And richly requite arrogant men' (Moffatt).

Day 3. Ps. xxxii.

David's account of his spiritual experience after his great sin.

(1) How does David describe the miseries of a guilty conscience? See verses 3, 4.

(2) What is the indispensable condition of forgiveness? Cf. Pr. xxviii. 13.

(3) What three great blessings does the forgiven soul receive, filling the heart with joy? But what two conditions of their enjoyment are laid down? See verses 5-11.

Notes.—(1) Verses 1, 2. See Rom. iv. 6-8.

(2) Verse 3. 'When I kept silence'; i.e. about my sin.

(3) Note the R.V. readings in verses 6 and 9.

Day 4. Ps. xxxiii.

This psalm begins where Ps. xxxii left off. The Hebrew word translated 'rejoice' in verse 1 is the same as that translated 'shout for joy' in xxxii. 11. The structure of the psalm is as follows: verses 1-3, introductory call to praise; verses 4-19, reasons why the Lord is to be praised; verses 20-22, concluding response of faith.

(1) How many reasons can you find in verses 4-11 why the Lord should be praised?

(2) Verse 12 is the central verse of the psalm. What reasons are given in verses 13-19 why the nation whose God is the Lord is blessed above other nations?

(3) In view of all that is said in verses 4-19 does your heart join in the call to praise of verses 1-3 and the declaration and prayer of verses 20-22?

Note.—Verse 3. 'A new song'; the song of the redeemed. See Ps. xl. 3. 'Play skilfully'. *Verb. sap.* for all who aspire to lead the praises of God's people.

Day 5. Ps. xxxiv.

This is an alphabetic psalm like Ps. xxv. For the circumstances, see the psalm title or heading and also 1 Sa. xxi. 12-xxii. 2. The psalm shines with a new light when regarded as composed in the cave of Adullam for the instruction of David's followers. The analysis is as follows: verses 1-3, call to praise; verses 4-7, four instances of Jehovah's deliverance; verses 8-10, an invitation to make personal trial of the way of faith; verses 11-14, what life in the fear of Jehovah means; verses 15-17, the principles underlying this philosophy of life; verses 18-21, the question of afflictions raised and answered. Verse 22 sums up the teaching of the psalm and points forward to the New Testament.

(1) Who are those who may expect the Lord's blessings? Note the various ways in which they are described. Are we ourselves entitled to claim blessing on the same grounds?

(2) Make a numbered list (avoiding repetition) of the blessings God gives to His people, as stated in this psalm.

Day 6. Ps. xxxv.

(1) The psalm falls into three divisions, each ending with a promise to give God thanks. Discover these sections, and give to each an appropriate heading, summarizing its contents.

(2) David gives a vivid picture of the vigour, subtlety and malice of his persecutors and reacts against them with equal vigour. What is the main cry of his heart, and on what grounds does he plead? In what respects is he an example to us?

Notes.—(1) Verses 4-6. Concerning this and similar prayers in the Psalms, see the *New Bible Handbook*, p. 196.

(2) Verses 11 and 12. See R.V. Malicious insinuations were made against David, which had never even entered his mind. Cf. 1 Sa. xxiv. 9, 17.

(3) Verse 13 (last clause). A difficult phrase of uncertain meaning. It seems to indicate heartfelt prayer, possibly repeated prayer.

Day 7. Ps. xxxvi.

(1) What are the principles of ungodly living and what its fruits? See verses 1-4.

(2) How different the character of God! Which of His attributes are here extolled, and what blessings flow from them? Are we living in the enjoyment of these blessings? See verses 5-9.

(3) To what twofold prayer do the Psalmist's reflections give rise and what vision is given him of the final end of those who work iniquity?

Note.—Verses 1 and 2. It seems best to regard transgression as personified, and as speaking in the heart of the evil man. The verses may then be translated as follows:

> 'Transgression uttereth its oracle to the wicked within his heart,
> For it flattereth him in his eyes
> That his iniquity shall not be found out and be hated'.

See r.v. and r.v. mg.

Week 38. Psalms XXXVII–XLI

Day 1. Ps. xxxvii. 1-20.

The psalm is alphabetic, each two successive lines commencing with a new letter, except that in three instances (verses 7, 20, 34) three lines are grouped under one letter, and in three instances (verses 14, 15; 25, 26; 39, 40) five lines.

'The same fundamental ideas recur throughout; but four symmetrical divisions of 11, 9, 11, and 9 verses respectively, in each of which a particular thought is prominent, may be observed' (*Camb. Bible*). These divisions are verses 1-11, 12-20, 21-31, 32-40. The first two form today's portion.

(1) Verses 1-11. What counsels are given in these verses? Under what two main heads may they be summed up, and what promises are made if these counsels be observed?

(2) Verses 12-20. How does this section amplify verses 2, 9, and 10 of the first section? Though the wicked seem to prosper, and the righteous seem to suffer loss, how have the righteous the advantage in the end?

Notes.—(1) Verses 3 and 4. There is some uncertainty in these two verses as to what is counsel, and what is promise. But it seems best to follow the r.v. in verse 3, and the r.v. mg. in verse 4.

(2) Note the changes in the r.v., especially in verses 10 and 20.

Day 2. Ps. xxxvii. 21-40.

(1) Verses 21-31. This third section of the psalm expands in fuller measure what was said of the reward of the righteous in the first section in verses 4, 6, 9, 11. What does this third section say about the righteous?

(2) Verses 32-40. How would you state in your own words the contrast between the righteous and the wicked, as summed up in this closing section?

(3) Why *must* there be this difference in the destiny of the two classes? See e.g. verses 22, 23, 24, 28, 39, 40; and cf. Ps. xxxiv. 15, 16.

Notes.—(1) Note the R.V. changes, especially in verses 35, 36 and 40.

(2) Verses 37 and 38. The word translated 'end' may be rendered 'posterity' (see R.V. mg.) and this was probably the thought in the Psalmist's mind. His vision was limited to life on earth; but in the light of the New Testament our eyes look beyond life here to the final 'end' in the life to come.

Day 3. Ps. xxxviii.

(1) The three divisions of the psalm are marked by the fact that they all begin with an address to God. Do you discern a progress in faith from one section to the next?

(2) If this psalm was written when David's great sin first came to light and struck dismay and horror into the hearts of his friends, can we wonder that its tone is so subdued? How great the contrast with Ps. xxxv! What light does the psalm throw upon the effects of discovered sin in the life of a believer?

Notes.—(1) Verse 5. 'My wounds'; i.e. my stripes, a poetic description of God's scourging.

(2) Verse 11. 'My sore'; better as in R.V., 'my plague'. His friends regard him with horror as if he were a leper.

(3) Verse 14. 'Reproofs'; better, 'arguments' as in R.V. mg., i.e. arguments in self-defence.

(4) Verse 20b. 'Because, etc.'; better, 'for my following of good'. The meaning is 'although I have sought to do good to them'. Cf. Ps. xxxv. 12-14.

Day 4. Ps. xxxix.

(1) Why was the Psalmist at first silent, and why did he break silence and speak? When he gave utterance to his thoughts, to whom did he speak? What may we learn from him in this? Cf. Ps. lxii. 8b; Jas. iii. 5, 6.

(2) What truths had been revealed to the Psalmist about our life on earth, and about man? Would you say that a realization of these same truths is very much needed in our land today? Cf. Mt. vi. 31-33; Lk. xii. 13-21.

(3) What does the psalm reveal as to the only safe place for confidence, and on what special ground does the Psalmist come to this conclusion?

Notes.—(1) Verse 6. See R.V. mg.

(2) Verse 8. Behind all that is said in the psalm lay the consciousness of transgressions. God used David's fall to open his eyes to many things.

(3) Verse 11. 'Like a moth'; read as in R.V. mg. It is God who is compared to a moth (cf. Ho. v. 12).

(4) Verse 12. 'As the strangers and sojourners among them were specially commended to the care of Israel (Ex. xxii. 21, etc.), he would plead to be treated by God with a corresponding clemency' (*Camb. Bible*).

Day 5. Ps. xl. 1-10.

This psalm, like Ps. xxvii, consists of two parts, which differ widely in their content. The first part is full of joyous thanksgiving for recent deliverance; the second pleads for help in the midst of distress and danger.

(1) What five things does David say in verses 1-3 that God did for him, and what effect did his deliverance have upon those who witnessed it? Cf. Acts ix. 35, 42.

(2) To what reflections, resolve, and actions did his deliverance give rise in David's own heart and life? See verses 4-10.

(3) Reading the psalm in the light of the New Testament compare especially verses 1-3 with Eph. ii. 1-10, and verses 6-8 with Heb. x. 4-10.

Notes.—(1) Verses 6-8 are quoted in Heb. x. 5-7, but from the LXX version, which has a different reading in the second line of verse 6. The general meaning is not, however, essentially different. 'As the ear is the instrument for receiving the divine command, so the body is the instrument for fulfilling it' (*Camb. Bible*).

(2) Verse 9. 'Righteousness'; i.e. God's righteousness. Cf. verse 10.

Day 6. Ps. xl. 11-17.

(1) How would you describe in your own words the vivid picture of his condition given by the Psalmist in verse 12 (R.V.)?

(2) What does he do in his dire need, and with what result? What vision of victory does he see by faith? See verses 13-16.

(3) The vision gives place to the consciousness of present need (verse 17). But a great change has taken place. Contrast verse 17 with verse 12. What has caused the Psalmist's soul thus to find rest and peace?

Notes.—(1) Verse 11. Some make this verse the conclusion of the first part of the psalm, translating it thus: 'Thou, O Lord, wilt not restrain . . . shall continually, etc. . . .'

(2) Verses 13-17 are found again in the Psalter in Ps. lxx.

Day 7. Ps. xli.

This psalm seems to belong to the time of Absalom's rebellion (see verse 9 and 2 Sam. xvii. 1-3). If so, it would appear that David suffered from a severe illness at this time.

(1) What gives David cause for hope in verses 1-3? Cf. Pr. xiv. 21. Are we thus generous? Cf. Jas. ii. 14-16; 1 Jn. iii. 16-22.

(2) On the other hand, what reasons has he for anxiety? See verses 4-9.

(3) Amid 'fighting without and fear within' (2 Cor. vii. 5), how did his faith finally gain the victory?

Notes.—(1) Verse 1. David is here referring to himself though speaking in general terms.

(2) Verse 3b. Moffatt translates 'and brings him back to health', which is probably the right meaning. The Heb. text literally means 'Thou changest his lying down' (see R.V. mg.).

(3) Verse 11. This may allude to the failure of Ahitophel's counsel. See 2 Sa. xvii. 14, and Ps. iii. 5 (Note on p. 81).

I and II THESSALONIANS

INTRODUCTION

(*See New Bible Handbook, pp. 377-381*)

THESE two Epistles were written in Corinth during Paul's second missionary journey, and not long after the church in Thessalonica had been founded (Acts xvii. 1-10). The first was written upon Timothy's return from a visit to Thessalonica, and the second a few months later. They are among the most personal of the apostle's letters in the New Testament, and present a vivid picture both of himself and of his readers, while revealing also the marvellous results of his missionary work in the great heathen city, the capital of Macedonia.

The apostle was greatly encouraged by the report, which Timothy brought, of the church's steadfastness under persecution and of continued progress. But there were some matters that gave him concern, in particular the prevalence of erroneous views about the second advent. The chief theme of the two Epistles, therefore, is the second coming of Christ, which is shown to be a comfort in bereavement, a motive to patience, an inspiration to hope, a safeguard in temptation, a help to purity, a challenge to watchfulness, a ground of rejoicing, and a separating and sanctifying power. The apostle's great aim is summed up in 1 Thes. iii. 13.

ANALYSIS

1 Thessalonians

      i.   The founding of the church.
     ii.   Service for Christ.
iii–iv. 12.   Sanctification and the daily walk.
 iv. 13–v.   The second coming and Christian behaviour.

2 Thessalonians

i–ii. 12.   Further teaching about the second coming.
ii. 13–iii.   Final exhortations.

Week 39. 1 AND 2 THESSALONIANS

Day 1. 1 Thes. i.

(1) Verse 1. A new society had come into being in Thessalonica. How is it here described, what was its bond of union, and what its inestimable wealth?

(2) What light is thrown by this chapter upon the fact and meaning of conversion? How were the Thessalonians converted? What was the nature of the preaching, and what the character of the response?

(3) Gather out the outstanding features of the Christian life and character of these converts. Making all allowance for the difference in circumstances, is the Christian life of today of this character?

Notes.—(1) Verse 3. Their faith issued in good works, their love toiled on for others' good, their hope of Christ's return endured, as they lived in communion with Him who had become their God and Father. Cf. Heb. xi. 27b.

(2) Verse 5. 'In much assurance'; better, 'with full conviction' (r.s.v.), that is, complete conviction on the part of the preachers as to the truth of their message.

Day 2. 1 Thes. ii.

(1) Verses 1-12. The real Paul. What does he here say of the aim, method, and spirit of his life and service? Make a list of the various points, those that show what he was not, and those which show what he was. As you ponder the list, what strikes you most forcibly?

(2) Verses 13, 14. What further light is here thrown upon the conversion of the Thessalonians, and upon conversion in general? Many hear the word of the gospel without being converted. What made the difference in the case of these Thessalonians?

(3) Verses 15-20. What two attitudes to missionary preaching are here set in contrast? Are you seeking to win others, and can you enter at all in experience into what Paul speaks of in verse 20?

Notes.—(1) Verse 2. Cf. Acts xvi. 19-24. 'Bold in our God'—note the source of their courage. 'With much contention.' Better, 'in the face of great opposition' (R.S.V.).
(2) Verse 7. Read as in R.V.
(3) Verse 18. He who engages in the work of the gospel will meet the opposition of Satan. Cf. Mk. iv. 15; 1 Thes. iii. 5.

Day 3. 1 Thes. iii.

(1) How is persecution regarded in this chapter (a) in relation to its inevitability (cf. Jn. xvi. 33), and (b) in relation to the spiritual peril which accompanies it (cf. 1 Pet. v. 8, 9)?
(2) It had been no easy thing for Paul to let Timothy go to Thessalonica (verses 1, 2), but now he had his reward. What two facts reported by Timothy gave him special comfort and joy? See verses 6-8 and cf. 3 Jn. 4.
(3) What twofold prayer, for himself and for his converts, did Paul pray? Note its intensity, and urgency, and, as regards his converts, what things he desires for them and the fulness of his prayer. Note, too, how it was accompanied with thanksgiving (verse 9; Phil. iv. 6; Col. iv. 2). What lessons may we learn from it about our own praying?

Notes.—(1) Verse 1. Cf. Acts xvii. 15.
(2) Verse 6. 'But now when Timotheus came'; better, as in R.V., 'But when Timothy came even now.' Paul wrote immediately.

Day 4. 1 Thes. iv.

(1) What three aspects of Christian living are emphasized in verses 1-12, and on what grounds?
(2) Why does the apostle go on reiterating the charge not only to practise mutual love and holiness, but to *increase* 'and *abound*' in these things? See iii. 12, iv. 1, 10, and compare Phil. iii. 12-14. Is not this counsel most necessary also today? Have we progressed in sanctification since our conversion?
(3) Verses 13-18. What practical use does Paul make here of the fact of the Lord's return (cf. iv. 18, v. 11) and what revelation does he give regarding it? State in your own words just what he says will happen.

Notes.—(1) Verse 8. 'Who hath also given unto us his holy Spirit'; better, as in R.V., 'Who giveth his Holy Spirit unto you'. The indwelling Holy Spirit is the seal of God's ownership, the evidence that we are His. See Eph. i. 13; Rom. viii. 9b. It is by the power of the Spirit that we overcome the flesh. See Gal. v. 16.

(2) Verses 11, 12. Read 'to aspire to live quietly, to mind your own affairs, and to work with your hands, as we charged you; so that you may command the respect of outsiders, and be dependent on nobody' (R.S.V.). Cf. 2 Thes. iii. 10-12; Eph. iv. 28.

Day 5. 1 Thes. v.

(1) Verses 1-11. How will the 'day of the Lord' break upon the world, and what will it mean (a) for men in general, and (b) for the people of Christ? Cf. Mt. xxiv. 32-44; Lk. xxi. 28.

(2) What is the difference between Christians and non-Christians as described in these verses? In view of the Lord's return, and the coming of 'the day of the Lord', how should Christians live?

(3) Make your own list of the injunctions in v. 12-22. If we say, 'Who is sufficient for these things', what is Paul's answer?

Notes.—(1) Verse 2. 'The day of the Lord'; an Old Testament phrase, signifying God's future intervention in history in salvation and judgment (Is. ii. 12, xiii. 6; Zp. i. 14, iii. 11, 16), and applied in the New Testament to the second coming of Christ (Lk. xvii. 24; 1 Cor. i. 8, etc.).

(2) Verse 6. 'Let us not sleep'; the word 'sleep' is used in this passage in three meanings; in this verse in the sense of spiritual insensibility, in verse 7 in the meaning of natural sleep, and in verse 10 in the sense of physical death, as in iv. 14, 15 (cf. iv. 16, 'the dead in Christ').

(3) Verse 12. 'Know'; in the sense of 'hold in respect', 'appreciate'.

(4) Verse 22. 'Appearance'; better, 'form', as in R.V.

Day 6. 2 Thes. i-ii. 12.

(1) Compare and contrast chapter i of this Epistle with chapter i of the first Epistle. What resemblances do you find and what differences?

(2) How is Christ's coming a comfort to persecuted Christians, and a terror to the unconverted? Contrast what is said by the apostle as to the final end of those who do not, and those who do, obey the gospel. What is his prayer for the latter? Are you seeking that this prayer may be fulfilled in you?

(3) Without going into the complicated question as to who 'the man of sin' is, consider his methods, his motives, his influences, and power, and his end, that we may see sin in its full manifestation in a human life, and realize how hateful it is. Observe also who are deceived by 'the man of sin'.

Notes.—(1) i. 5. 'A manifest token of the righteous judgment of God'. The reference is to their faith and patience, which is a clear indication of what the righteous judgment of God will be, namely, that they will be accounted worthy. Cf. Lk. xx. 35.

(2) i. 6. 'If so be that' (R.V.); better, 'since indeed' (R.S.V.).

(3) i. 7, 8. Cf. Mk. viii. 38; Is. lxvi. 15; Je. x. 25.

(4) ii. 1. 'By the coming'; better, 'concerning the coming' (R.S.V.).

(5) ii. 2. 'Spirit'; prophetic utterance: 'word'; reasoned discourse (cf. verse 15). 'The day of Christ is at hand'; better, 'has come' (R.S.V.).

(6) ii. 12. 'Damned'; better, 'condemned' (R.S.V.).

Day 7. 2 Thes. ii. 13–iii.

(1) Consider how in ii. 13, 14 the whole work of salvation is summarized. What is its origin, what are the means God uses, what is man's part and what the final end?

(2) What three prayers does Paul pray in this portion, and what prayer does he ask for himself? With iii. 16 cf. Jn. xiv. 27, xvi. 33; Phil. iv. 6, 7.

(3) What defect in the church's life does Paul rebuke, and what directions does he give to remedy it?

Notes.—(1) iii. 2, 3. From the unbelief of men the apostle turns to the faithfulness of the Lord.

(2) iii. 5. 'Patient waiting'; better, 'patience' (R.V.) or 'steadfastness' (R.S.V.). The heart is apt to wander. May the Lord guide it into the abiding place of God's love and Christ's patience!

JOB

INTRODUCTION

(See New Bible Handbook, pp. 186-191)

THE book of Job shows us a good man overwhelmed by appalling calamities and physical suffering, struggling to reconcile his own experience and his honest observation of human life in general with faith in God's justice.

The author of the book is unknown, and even the date is uncertain. But the entire absence of any reference to Israel and the patriarchal civilization described favour an early date. It is possible that the book is an inspired drama rather than a literal history, but it is certain from Ezk. xiv. 14 and Jas. v. 11 that it was at least founded on historical fact.

This book is valuable for its warnings and its positive teaching. It warns us, by the example of the friends of Job, how not to deal with those in sorrow or in intellectual or spiritual difficulty. It emphasizes the necessity of honesty in defence of truth (xiii. 4-12; xlii. 7). It displays an unparalleled example of faith in God against all appearances; for, despite a few temporary lapses, Job does maintain his faith, appealing from the seeming injustice of God's dealings to the just God who must exist somewhere, if only He could be found.

In the speeches of Elihu, but still more in the preface and ending, the book suggests reasons why God's own people may have to pass through suffering. Job himself has a momentary glimpse of the answer to this problem (xxiii. 10). The divine speeches and Job's reaction to them reveal to us that the true solution to all difficulties about the ways of God is not argument, but contact with the Lord Himself. Jehovah does not enter into argument with Job, but simply displays Himself, and Job is wholly satisfied.

The book is also remarkable in its prophetic aspect. Job, in his pathetic gropings after God, cries out for an Arbitrator between God and himself, who might lay His hand on both. And though the very heart of his problem was the absence of belief in a future life which would redress the inequalities of the present, he is first led to wish that there might be another life (xiv. 13-15) and later he rises on the wings of faith and inspiration to a positive statement that one day his Redeemer would stand upon the earth, and that after his own body had been destroyed he would see God (xix. 25-27).

ANALYSIS

N.B.—It is particularly important in studying the book of Job to use the Revised Version. The translation is much clearer, and the following notes and questions are based upon it.

Week 40. JOB I–XIV
Day 1. Job i–iii.

(1) i–ii. 10. What does this portion reveal concerning (a) Job's character; (b) the measure of his calamities; and (c) the reason why such a man was permitted to suffer so greatly?

(2) ii. 11–iii. What caused Job, who had hitherto maintained a faith undismayed (i. 21; ii. 10), to break out in the anguished cry of chapter iii?

THE FIRST CYCLE OF SPEECHES (IV–XIV)
Job's terrible sufferings, which his friends had now watched in silence for seven days, produced in him, and in them, a very different reaction. Holding firmly to the current doctrine that suffering is inflicted by God because of sin (and in proportion to the sin), they concluded that Job must have committed grievous sins, though they believed also that by confessing and forsaking these he might be restored to the divine favour. They therefore urged him to repent. Job resented their attitude. Conscious of his integrity, he found in his sufferings an insoluble enigma; and under the torment of his pain, made bitter complaint against God's treatment of him.

Day 2. Job iv and v. First speech of Eliphaz.

(1) iv. 1-11. Eliphaz expresses surprise at Job's despair. What, in his view, should Job have remembered?

(2) iv. 12–v. 7. What truth was brought home to Eliphaz in a vision? And how did it show him that suffering is inevitable for weak, sinful, man (iv. 19–v. 1), and that murmuring is foolish (v. 2-5)?

(3) v. 8-27. What course does Eliphaz recommend to Job (see v. 8 and 17), and what does he promise to Job if he will follow it?

Notes.—(1) iv. 10, 11 are an illustration of the fate of the wicked.

(2) v. 6, 7. The meaning is that affliction does not come without cause. Man's nature, being prone to evil, draws trouble upon him. Cf. iv. 8.

Day 3. Job vi and vii. Job's reply to Eliphaz.

Job draws attention first to the greatness of his sufferings (vi. 1-13), then he expresses keen disappointment at the attitude of his friends (vi. 14-30). Finally, swept away by the contemplation of his misery, he flings question after question upon God (vii).

(1) What insight do we get in Job's words into the intensity of longing which one who is undergoing great suffering has for understanding and sympathy? Have you ever disappointed a friend because of a lack of this? See especially vi. 14.

(2) By what four images does Job in vii. 1-10 describe his life?

(3) How do Job's questions addressed to God in vii. 12-21 help us to understand his problem?

Notes.—(1) vi. 13. 'No, there is no help, none; and all aid has abandoned me' (Moffatt).

(2) vi. 27. Job accuses his friends of being as heartless as those who would cast lots for a fatherless child or bargain over a friend.

Day 4. Job viii–ix. 24. First speech of Bildad and Job's reply.

(1) Bildad gives essentially the same view of God and the same counsel as Eliphaz did. To whom does he appeal for confirmation of his teaching?

(2) Bildad's harsh cocksureness drives Job almost to distraction. Bildad had said that if Job were pure and upright surely God would awake for him (viii. 6), but Job's whole problem is that he is pure and upright, and God, on the contrary, attacked him. How, he asks, can man get his rights in such a case (ix. 2, see note below)? To what very different conception of God does Job give expression in ix. 3-24?

Notes.—(1) viii. 11-13. As the papyrus and reed grass (R.V. mg.) wither when deprived of soil and water, so the wicked, losing God's favour, will suddenly perish. Other images of the downfall of the wicked are given in verses 14b-15, and 16-19.

(2) ix. 2. The meaning here is, How will man establish his righteousness before God?

(3) ix. 13, 14. Rahab is here probably another name for 'dragon' (cf. Is. i. 9). The argument is, If the dragon fought in vain against God, how much ess shall I prevail?

Day 5. Job ix. 25–x. Job's reply (continued).

Obsessed with the idea that God is determined to hold him guilty, Job is unable to rise above his misery (ix. 25-31), and longs that God were human like himself, or that there were some umpire between them (ix. 33, R.V. mg.). In chapter x he again seeks to discover why God treats him thus, and comes to the desperate conclusion that this is God's real nature (x. 13).

(1) How has Job's longing, expressed in ix. 32-35, been met in the Lord Jesus? See 1 Tim. ii. 5; Heb. iv. 15.

(2) Do you think God was displeased by Job's boldness? See xxxviii. 2; xl. 8, but also xlii. 7. Cf. Ps. lxii. 8b; 1 Sa. i. 9-18.

Notes.—(1) ix. 35. 'Inwardly I have no guilty fears' (Moffatt).

(2) x. 10-15. Job's conception of God, under the pressure of his sufferings, becomes temporarily distorted. He conceives that all God's care of him from his birth onwards was but a mask to hide His real purposes. God was such that if he sinned it would be marked against him; if he became a wicked man, woe betide him; and even if he were righteous, he must still hang his head.

Day 6. Job xi and xii. First speech of Zophar, and Job's reply.

To Zophar Job's words seemed boastful and impious, and he administers a sharp reproof (xi. 1-6). Then, after a eulogy of God's wisdom (xi. 5-12), he urges Job to repent that he may be restored (xi. 13-20). His speech, however, only stirs Job to indignant remonstrances (xii. 1-10). How easy it is to try to improve an occasion without really understanding it! True doctrine, mistakenly applied, may exasperate rather than heal.

(1) What four steps in repentance does Zophar counsel Job to take? See xi. 13, 14. Consider also the beautiful picture which he draws of the blessings which will come to Job in consequence of repentance (xi. 15-19).

(2) In xii. 11-25 Job discourses on the wisdom and strength of God far more profoundly than Zophar had done. What examples of God's action does he cite?

Notes.—(1) xii. 4, 5. Job declares that it is only because he has .allen into misfortune that men dare to hold him in such contempt.

(2) xii. 12, 13. Verse 12 may be read as a question, 'With the aged wisdom?' meaning 'Do you say that wisdom is with the aged?' 'No! with *God* is wisdom.'

(3) xii. 18. 'He dismantles royalty, and drives kings off in chains' (Moffatt).

(4) xii. 22. No darkness is impenetrable to Him!

Day 7. Job xiii and xiv. Job's reply (continued).

After a further rebuke to his friends (xiii. 1-12), Job, as before in chapter vii, turns from them to God (xiii. 13-22), and pleads his cause before Him (xiii. 23-xiv). He mourns his desperate condition and approaching death (xiii. 23-xiv. 12), and then, suddenly, the arresting thought breaks upon him that there may be a life hereafter, in which he will be restored to God and fellowship. If it were so, he says, how patiently would he await that happy day! How joyfully respond to God's call! (xiv. 13-15). But the vision fades, and he bemoans again his hopeless outlook (xiv. 16-22).

(1) What may we learn from Job's rebuke to his friends of the responsibility of speaking to men on God's behalf? See xiii. 7-12 and xlii. 7, 8. Are we sufficiently watchful about this?

(2) Contrast the fleeting vision of a future life in xiv. 13-16 with the light and certainty of our Lord's word in Jn. xi. 25, 26. How does this whole chapter help us to understand the difference the gospel has made? See Rom. viii. 18; 2 Cor. iv. 17, 18.

Week 41. Job xv–xxxi

SECOND CYCLE OF SPEECHES (xv–xxi)

Job's friends had failed to persuade him to take the only course that seemed to them to offer a hope of his restoration. Their speeches, therefore, in this second cycle assume a harsher tone and contain no appeal to acknowledge his sin, but dwell on the character and fate of the wicked. Job at first is greatly oppressed by this fresh evidence that God and man alike are against him, but finally, in chapter xxi, he denies the accuracy of his friends' observations and arguments.

Day 1. Job xv–xvii. The second speech of Eliphaz, and Job's reply.

(1) Observe the severity of the words of Eliphaz as compared with his first speech. He was angry because Job did not behave as Eliphaz thought he ought to behave. Have you sometimes found yourself losing sympathy with those you seek to win, because they will not accept what seems to you so clear?

(2) Job's agony of mind is pitiful, yet he cleaves in spite of everything to God. What verses in chapters xvi and xvii show particularly the light of an unquenchable faith shining through Job's deep darkness?

Notes.—(1) xv. 4. Job's attitude, Eliphaz says, injures true religion.

(2) xv. 11b. A reference probably to his previous speech.

(3) xv. 12. 'Wink', i.e. flash in wrath.

(4) xv. 18, 19. Eliphaz claims that his doctrine is ancient and pure, untainted by foreign heresies.

(5) xvii. 2, 3. Turning from his friends, whom he calls 'mockers' (verse 2), Job pleads with God to undertake for him, for there is no one else who can do so.

(6) xvii. 13-16. Sheol is the place of the dead, conceived as a kind of prison under the earth with gates (xxxviii. 17), bars (xvii. 16), and keys (Rev. i. 18). Job affirms that the worm and corruption of the grave are now as near to him as his nearest relatives.

Day 2. Job xviii and xix. Second speech of Bildad, and Job's reply.

(1) Bildad tells Job that the fixed order of the world will not be overturned because he, Job, is angry (xviii. 1-4). In what five stages is the sinner's downfall described? See verses 5-6, 7-10, 11-14, 15-19, 20-21.

(2) Job is completely broken by the persistent assumption of his friends that he is wicked (xix. 1-5). Set upon by God (6-12) and forsaken by man (13-20), ought he not to be pitied by his friends (21, 22)? But in this darkest hour, to what grand assurance does his faith triumphantly rise?

Notes.—(1) xix. 23, 24. Job desires that his plea might be indelibly recorded, so that it might never be lost to sight. But even as he speaks, his faith grasps something far better (25-27).

(2) xix. 26. 'In my flesh' or 'without my flesh' (R.V. mg.).

(3) xix. 28, 29. Job warns his friends that if they persist in persecuting him, and in asserting that the cause of his sufferings is in himself (i.e. in his sins), they will suffer divine judgment.

Day 3. Job xx and xxi. Second speech of Zophar, and Job's reply.

(1) Zophar, hot with anger, makes known to Job truth old as time (xx. 1-4). What does he say about the sinner's prosperity

(5-11), the punishment that sin brings (12-22), and God's final judgments (23-29)?

(2) Zophar's speech stirs Job to give utterance to thoughts that fill his own mind with fear (xxi. 5, 6). The facts of life, he says, present a very different picture from that which Zophar has drawn. What, in fact, happens to the wicked in this life (7-34)?

(3) What charges does Job bring against his friends? See xxi. 22, 27, 34. What lay at the root of the difference between him and them?

Notes.—(1) xx. 11. 'When manly vigour fills his frame, he and his manly vigour go to dust' (Moffatt).

(2) xx. 23. See R.V. mg. The meaning seems to be that God will rain wrath upon the wicked as his food. Cf. Ps. xi. 6.

(3) xxi. 2. Job, in sarcasm, tells his friends that the best comfort they can give him is to listen to what he has to say.

(4) xxi. 13b. The wicked have no long, painful illness at death.

(5) xxi. 30. Read as in R.V. mg.

(6) xxi. 31. 'Whoever tells him plainly what he is? Whoever punishes him for his crimes?'

THIRD CYCLE OF SPEECHES (XXII–XXXI)

In this third cycle there is no speech from Zophar (see, however, xxvii. 7-23, note), and the speech of Bildad is very brief. Eliphaz first charges Job with specific sins—which Job later vehemently denies (xxxi)—and then makes a final appeal to him to 'return to the Almighty', who will forgive and bless.

Day 4. Job xxii–xxiv. Third speech of Eliphaz, and Job's reply.

(1) What blessings does Eliphaz say will come to the man who walks in God's favour? There are at least seven blessings enumerated. With verse 29 cf. Pr. xxiv. 16; Mt. xxiii. 12, and with verse 30, Jas. v. 16.

(2) Job insists upon his integrity, and longs that he might be able to lay his case before God (xxiii). What strange anomalies does he see, as he looks out upon the world? See xxiv. He can see no solution to the mystery. What light shines upon it for us in the New Testament? See Jn. v. 28, 29; Rom. ii. 4-11; Rev. xx. 11-15.

Notes.—(1) xxii. 2-4. The argument of Eliphaz is that God's treatment of men is not with a view to any gain or advantage to Himself, but for man's sake. Since we cannot suppose that He punishes them for piety (verse 4), it must be because of their sin.

(2) xxiii. 10. 'Yet He knows how I live; when He tests me, I shall prove sterling gold' (Moffatt).

(3) xxiv. 1. 'Times', 'days', i.e. times and days of judgment. Job's complaint is that the wicked seem to act unchecked.

(4) xxiv. 4b-17. Descriptions of (a) the sufferings of the outcast and op-

pressed people, and (b) those who work evil under cover of darkness (13-17).

(5) xxiv. 18-24. In verses 18-21 Job gives the orthodox view of what happens to the wicked, and in verses 22-24 he gives, in contrast, the true facts, as he himself sees them. Verse 22 should be read as in R.V. mg. Verse 24 has the same meaning as xxi. 13b; see note there.

Day 5. Job xxv–xxvii. 6. Third speech of Bildad, and Job's reply.

(1) What is Bildad's answer to Job's plea of personal uprightness? Would Job have dissented from the general fact of man's sinfulness? With verse 4 compare Job's words in xiii. 26, xiv. 4.

(2) Job knows God's greatness as well as Bildad. How does he describe it here, as it operates in the underworld of Sheol (xxvi. 5, 6) and in the heavens and the earth (xxvi. 7-13)? And how finally does he show how immeasurable God's greatness is? See verse 14.

(3) The knowledge of God's greatness does not, however, answer Job's problem—why the Almighty was dealing with him thus. What one thing is Job resolved to hold fast? See xxvii. 1-6. Was he right in this?

Day 6. Job xxvii. 7–xxviii.

(1) In what four ways is the wicked man's fate described in xxvii. 7-23? See verses 13-15, 16-18, 19-22, 23.

(2) What two kinds of wisdom are distinguished in chapter xxviii—the first known to God alone, the second belonging to man?

(3) How does the chapter show that the first kind of wisdom is not discoverable by man? And how is this conclusion modified in the New Testament? See 1 Cor. i. 30, ii. 7-16; Eph. i. 8-10.

Notes.—(1) xxvii. 7-23. These verses contradict what Job has just been saying in xxi and xxiv. They would be much more appropriate in the mouths of Job's friends, and are thought by some to be the third speech of Zophar which has become displaced.

(2) xxviii. 1-11. This is a description of mining operations. Miners open up the dark depths (verse 3), burrow underground and are forgotten by those who walk above them, and swing suspended in cages or on ropes (verse 4). Verse 5 gives a vivid contrast between agricultural operations on the surface of the earth and the work of miners underground. For verse 10 see R.V. mg.

(3) 'Wisdom in this passage, as in other parts of Scripture where it is spoken of, is properly the idea or conception lying behind or under the order of the universe—the world plan' (A. B. Davidson).

Day 7. Job xxix–xxxi. Final speech of Job.

(1) How does Job describe the contrast between his past and his present condition?

(2) Of what sins, secret and public, does Job here declare himself innocent? Make a list and use it for self-examination.

Notes.—(1) xxix. 7. The 'gate' and the 'street' (or 'broad place', r.v. mg.) signify the place of assembly of the city council.

(2) xxix. 24. See r.v. mg. The meaning is that Job encouraged others, who had lost confidence, while never losing his own joyousness.

(3) xxx. 2-15. Even the least and lowest of men now held Job in derision.

Week 42. Job XXXII–XLII

Day 1. Job xxxii and xxxiii. Introduction of Elihu, and his first speech.

Elihu was a younger man than Job's three friends, and appears to have been a silent listener to their discussions. Stirred by their failure to find an answer to Job, and still more by Job's own attitude, he essays to take speech himself. He has a profound reverence for God, and has been pained by Job's utterances. He emphasizes mainly two points: that God being what He is, He cannot be unjust nor can man contend with Him; and that the purpose of affliction is often to preserve men from sinning.

(1) On what grounds does Elihu, as a younger man, claim the right to speak? And in what spirit does he enter upon the discussion?

(2) In chapter xxxiii Elihu takes up the assertions that Job has made: the first, that God counted him as an enemy, though he was innocent (8-11); and the second, that God refused to hear and answer his appeal (13, see note). Elihu's answer to the first assertion is given in verse 12 and to the second in verses 13-20, where he argues that God does speak to man. In what ways does he say God speaks, and for what purpose?

Notes.—(1) xxxii. 13, 14. Elihu says the friends of Job must not ride away on the excuse that they had found an unlooked-for wisdom in Job, which God alone could overcome; Elihu believes that there is a reply to Job, and that he can give it.

(2) xxxiii. 6, 7. An allusion to Job's words in ix. 34, 35, xiii. 21.

(3) xxxiii. 13. 'Now why do you complain of Him for never answering your cry?' (Moffatt).

(4) xxxiii. 23, 24. 'One among a thousand', i.e. one of God's many angels. 'He' in verse 24 refers to God.

Day 2. Job xxxiv and xxxv. Elihu's second and third speeches.

These two chapters are closely connected, giving an answer to two further assertions which Job had made: first, that God was wronging him (xxxiv. 5, 6); and second, that there is no profit in drawing near to God (xxxiv. 9). The first assertion Elihu answers in chapter xxxiv, and the second in chapter xxxv. His first answer is that God, just because He is God, cannot be unjust (xxxiv. 10-12, cf. Gn. xviii. 25; Rom. iii. 5). He then develops this thought, viewing God first as Creator (verses 13-15) and second as Ruler (verses 17-30); and finally gives counsel to Job (verses 31-33, see note below) and condemns his attitude (verses 34-37). In regard to Job's second assertion, Elihu answers that man's conduct cannot affect God; it can affect only man (xxxv. 2-8).

(1) What do you think of Elihu's discourse in chapter xxxiv? If he was right in regard to God, was he not too severe in regard to Job? See especially verses 7, 8 and 35-37.

(2) God does deliver those who cry to Him, giving them songs in the night (xxxv. 10); if not, there is a reason. What reason does Elihu here suggest why the oppressed may cry for help in vain?

Notes.—(1) xxxiv. 14. The first clause may be rendered 'If He set his heart upon Himself'. The thought of verses 13-15 seems to be that God as Creator has no motive for injustice, and that the existence and preservation of the universe is an evidence of God's interest in His creatures.

(2) xxxiv. 17-19. 'Can any one opposed to justice govern? Would you denounce the strong God and the just, who tells a king he is a knave, tells nobles they are villains, who never favours princes, never prefers rich men to poor?' (Moffatt).

(3) xxxiv. 23-30. There is no need for God to act as men do by process of trial and judgment—an allusion to Job's words in xxiii. 3, 4. God knows all, and acts at once.

(4) xxxiv. 31a. 'No, tell God' (Moffatt)—an advice to Job to confess his error.

Day 3. Job xxxvi and xxxvii. Fourth speech of Elihu.

(1) xxxvi. 1-25. In this first part of his speech Elihu gives further description of God's just and beneficent rule, and urges Job to humble himself before Him ere it be too late. What does Elihu say as to the purpose of affliction?

(2) xxxvi. 26-xxxvii. To what manifestation of God's greatness does Elihu here draw attention? And to what conclusion does he seek to lead Job?

Notes.—(1) xxxvii. 7. 'That keep men within doors . . . to let all mortals feel His power' (Moffatt). Verse 6 should end with a comma, not a full stop.

(2) xxxvii. 20. Elihu expresses dread at the thought of contending with God.

Day 4. Job xxxviii–xl. 5. God answers Job out of the storm.

With much of what Elihu said Job was no doubt in agreement, though his problem had not been solved, and his mind was not quieted to listen to the voice of God Himself, as He comes to deliver and bless His tried and faithful servant. God first challenges Job to stand up to Him, as Job had often said he wished to do (xxxviii. 3, cf. xiii. 3, xxiii. 3, 4, xxxi. 37).

(1) God presents before Job a picture of some of the wonders of earth and sky (xxxviii. 1-38) and then a picture of some of the marvels of animal life, accompanied throughout by humbling

questions bringing out Job's littleness in comparison with God. Why did God speak thus rather than remove Job's perplexities? Was it because Job *needed* to be humbled? Cf. xxxviii. 2.

(2) What was the effect upon Job? See xl. 3-5.

Notes.—(1) xxxviii. 13. Cf. xxiv. 16, 17.

(2) xl. 5. 'Once . . . twice'. 'Hebrew idiom for a number of times'.

Day 5. Job xl. 6–xli. God answers Job out of the storm a second time.

In His first revelation God had rebuked Job for his presumption in desiring to contend with Him; but Job had gone further, and, in upholding his own righteousness had cast doubt upon God's righteousness, both in regard to himself as an individual and in His governance of the world. God now speaks to Job on this point, ironically inviting Job to act as God and show that his own right hand can save him (xl. 6-14).

(1) Having called upon Job to array himself with honour and majesty (xl. 10), He brings before him two powerful wild creatures —the hippopotamus (xl. 15-24) and the crocodile (xli)—and bids him observe them closely. Try to picture them as here described.

(2) What does God intend that Job should learn from these animals? What questions does He ask Job?

Notes.—(1) xl. 19b. See R.V. mg. The 'sword' may refer to the tusks.

(2) xli. 9. 'The hope of him', i.e. the hope of catching him.

(3) xli. 13. 'His outer garment', i.e. his scaly armour. 'His double bridle' may refer to the two corners of his jaws.

Day 6. Job xlii.

(1) What brought Job to the deep humbling and self-abasement described in verses 1-6? Was it the argument which God used, or was it rather just the fact that God had appeared and had spoken with him? Unbelief vanished in the light of God's countenance, and Job's heart found rest, even though the *reason* of his sufferings had not yet been explained to him.

(2) How do Job's friends show themselves to have been true men of God, though bound by doctrinal prejudice? Read the closing verses of the book in the light of Jas. v. 11 and 16.

Day 7. Revision.

Note down the main lessons which you have learned from the reading of the book of Job. What, in particular, does it teach about suffering in its purpose and in its effects?

PROVERBS

INTRODUCTION

(See New Bible Handbook, pp. 186, 198-200)

PROVERBS i. 7 provides the key to the Book and to the whole of the Wisdom Literature (Job, Proverbs, Ecclesiastes). It all starts from the creed of one God—Jehovah—and wisdom is to know and do His will. The term 'proverb' has the double meaning of a short parable and a pithy saying.

The Proverbs are all intensely practical, covering the human race and the whole of its activity, aiming at giving 'knowledge and discretion', or the building up of the 'perfect man', by fixing truth in the memory. As expressing eternal spiritual principles many of them can receive their full meaning only when applied to the believer in Christ.

ANALYSIS

i–ix.	The appeal of wisdom.
x–xxii. 16.	Proverbs (grouped in various ways).
xxii. 17–xxiv.	Second collection, headed 'Words of the Wise.'
xxv–xxix.	Third collection, ascribed to Solomon.
xxx, xxxi.	Words of Agur and Lemuel.

Week 43. PROVERBS I–XI. 13.

Day 1. Pr. i.

(1) From the expressed purpose of the book in verses 1-6, what personal profit may we expect from studying it?

(2) Contrast the enticement of sinners with the call of wisdom. What will be the end in each case of following the one and rejecting the other?

(3) How may we apply the words of wisdom in verses 22-33 to our Lord Jesus Christ? See, e.g., Mt. vii. 13-27; Lk. xix. 41-44.

Note.—The word translated 'simple' is used in Proverbs in the sense of inexperienced and credulous, and hence unwary and easily led astray. Cf. xiv. 15.

Day 2. Pr. ii and iii.

(1) What directions are given in these chapters for the attaining of wisdom? Make a list of them as a guide to your own life.

(2) What benefits does wisdom bring us, and from what evils does it preserve us? How far have we proved this in our own experience?

(3) 'My son'. What application does the writer of the Epistle to the Hebrews give to these words? See Heb. xii. 5-10.

Day 3. Pr. iv and v.

(1) What are the main lessons that the speaker seeks in these chapters to impress upon us? What measure of heed have we given and are we giving to these most urgent counsels? Cf. Lk. viii. 18.

(2) iv. 23-27 provide an admirable guide to successful living. Cf. verse 18. Heart, lips, eyes, feet; what directions are given concerning each?

(3) What is the end of those who neglect this way of wisdom? See iv. 19, v. 9-14, v. 21-23.

Notes.—(1) iv. 24. 'Froward' means twisted, crooked, and perverse—forsaking the paths of truth.

(2) v. 6 and 14. The meaning in both verses is obscure. Verse 6 is translated by Moffatt thus: 'The high road of life is not for her, shifty and slippery are her tracks.' Verse 14 may mean, 'I had well-nigh come to complete grief in the congregation and assembly.'

Day 4. Pr. vi and vii.

(1) Verses 1-5 give warning against foolish financial commitments and pledges. What other warnings are given in these chapters?

(2) In what forms do the sins here spoken of manifest themselves at the present day?

(3) Test your life in the light of vi. 16-19.

Notes.—(1) vi. 1. 'Stricken thy hand'; a method of giving a pledge, cf. 2 Ki. x. 15. Suretyship, frequently condemned in Proverbs, held grave dangers, because of the responsibility resting upon the surety, and the penalties to which he was liable. Cf. Gn. xliii. 9.

(2) vi. 13 describes the secret, clandestine ways of the evil-minded man.

Day 5. Pr. viii. 1-31.

This passage should be read in the R.V., especially verses 22, 23.

(1) Contrast the description of wisdom with that of the woman in vii. 5-27. How do they differ in speech, in conduct, in what they offer, and the goal to which they lead their followers?

(2) What is said of wisdom in verses 22-31 concerning (a) her existence from the beginning; (b) her part in creation; (c) her communion with God; (d) her interest in man? Consider how in all these respects there is here a dim foreshadowing of Christ. See, e.g. (a) Jn. xvii. 5; (b) Jn. i. 1-3; Col. i. 15-17; (c) Mt. xi. 27; (d) Heb. ii. 17, 18.

(3) What sayings in this portion grip you most strongly?

Day 6. Pr. viii. 32–ix.

(1) What similar but still greater gifts than those which wisdom offers in viii. 32-36 are offered in Christ? See, e.g., Mt. xi. 29; Lk. xi. 28; Jn. xiv. 21, xvii. 2, 3, iii. 36.

(2) Set ix. 1-6 and ix. 13-18 side by side. In what respects are wisdom and folly (ix. 13, R.V. mg.) alike, and wherein do they differ?

Day 7. Pr. x–xi. 13.

(1) In x. 2-6 there are four conditions of wellbeing in circumstances, mind, and character. What are they?

(2) In the light of Jas. iii. 10, what uses of the faculty of speech in this chapter are (a) commended, (b) to be avoided?

(3) What will the possession of integrity secure for a man (xi. 1-13)?

Week 44. PROVERBS XI. 14–XXII. 16.

Day 1. Pr. xi. 14–xii.

(1) What two kinds of sin or sinners are said in this passage to be an abomination unto the Lord?

(2) What other sins are here condemned? In what verses are they traced to their origin in the *heart*? Cf. iv. 23; Mt. xii. 34, 35, xv. 18, 19.

(3) Apply to yourself the five principles for the using of money expressed in xi. 24-28.

Day 2. Pr. xiii–xiv. 21.

(1) 'Considering the issue of their life' (Heb. xiii. 7, R.V.). What is said in today's portion concerning the issues of their life in the case of the righteous and of the wicked respectively?

(2) Gather out what is taught about 'fools' and 'folly'. What, in contrast, should the manner of our life, if we are wise, be (a) in relation to the Word, (b) in relation to our neighbours, and (c) in conduct and speech?

Day 3. Pr. xiv. 22–xv. 23.

(1) What is said in today's portion about the beneficent effects of right words?

(2) What is said about 'the Lord'? How may we discern the fear of the Lord in our own hearts?

(3) Can we claim to have the five things making for satisfaction which are enumerated in xv. 13-17?

Day 4. Pr. xv. 24–xvi.

(1) How does xv. 24-33 illustrate what has been called 'the sanity of religion'?

(2) Gather out what is said in today's portion about the Lord, and about man's proper attitude to Him.

(3) Consider in xvi. 27-30 the multiplied evil wrought by evil men. Cf. Ps. xcvii. 10.

Day 5. Pr. xvii and xviii.

(1) Gather out the sins condemned in chapter xvii.

(2) What reasons are given in chapter xviii why we should 'watch the door of our lips'?

(3) Consider the two fortresses in xviii. 10, 11; and compare Jn. x. 27, 28; Lk. xii. 15-21.

Note.—xviii. 10. 'The Name of the Lord' denotes the character of God Himself, as revealed to us in the Scriptures. See ,e.g., Ex. xxxiv. 5, 7. For us it is summed up in 'Jesus'.

Day 6. Pr. xix–xx. 13.

(1) Make a list of the varied conditions and circumstances in respect to which counsel is given in today's portion. Which of them apply more particularly to yourself?

(2) What is said about the Lord? Show how the fact of His presence forms the foundation on which the writer's counsels are based.

(3) Have you found a 'faithful man' (xx. 6)? Do others find such a man in you? Cf. Rev. xvii. 14.

Day 7. Pr. xx. 14–xxii. 16.

(1) In xx. 17-25 what different kinds of action are to be avoided?

(2) xx. 24 speaks of God's sovereignty, and xx. 27 of man's responsibility. What other verses in today's portion touch on these two complementary truths?

(3) Gather out from today's portion those principles for wise living that most impress you.

Notes.—(1) xx. 27. 'The spirit of man'; here a synonym for 'the conscience'. 'All the innermost parts of the belly' is a Hebrew idiom for the whole inward being. Cf. verse 30.

(2) xxi. 4. The meaning of the word 'plowing' (R.V. 'lamp') is uncertain.

(3) xxii. 16. 'He that giveth to the rich'; that is, to gain favour.

Week 45. PROVERBS XXII. 17–XXXI

Day 1. Pr. xxii. 17–xxiii.

A new series of aphorisms begins here, extending to the end of chapter xxiv and divided into two parts (xxii. 17–xxiv. 22 and xxiv. 23-34).

(1) What counsels already given in earlier chapters are repeated in today's portion?

(2) What are the marks of a wise 'son' (xxiii. 15)? What will he avoid, and what will he practise?

(3) What, according to xxiii. 29-35, are the effects of too much indulgence in wine?

Notes.—(1) xxiii. 6-8. 'Him that hath an evil eye'; that is, a niggard. The meaning of verse 7a is not clear. A possible rendering is 'For as he dealeth (stingily) with himself, so he deals with thee.'

(2) Verse 14. 'From hell'; better, as in R.V., 'from Sheol'; i.e. from an early death.

Day 2. Pr. xxiv.

(1) What missionary call is heard in verses 11, 12? Are we saying concerning those who are going down to death, 'Behold, we knew it not'?

(2) What other instructions are given? Make a list of them.

(3) What did the wise (verse 23) learn from the field of the sluggard? What references have been made to slothfulness in earlier chapters? See also xxii. 13, xxvi. 16.

Notes.—(1) Verse 26. 'He kisseth the lips'; the meaning is, 'He shows love'. Moffatt translates: 'He is a true friend who is honest with you.'

(2) Verse 27. First acquire the means to set up house, and then marry and build.

Day 3. Pr. xxv–xxvi. 12.

(1) How does our Lord in one of His parables adapt the teaching of xxv. 6, 7?

(2) Observe in xxv. 8-25 how many illustrations are given of the power and influence of words both to do good and to do harm. Are we sufficiently careful in this matter?

(3) In what ways does the passage xxvi. 1-12 enforce the familiar injunction 'Don't be a fool'? Among whom did Christ find 'fools'? See Mt. vii. 26, xxiii. 17, xxv. 2; Lk. xi. 40, xii. 20, xxiv. 25.

Note.—The 'fool' is one who is wilfully unresponsive to the teaching of divine wisdom, and going his own self-chosen way, hurts himself and others.

Day 4. Pr. xxvi. 13–xxvii.

(1) What various kinds of wrong speech are exposed in xxvi. 18–xxvii. 2?

(2) 'My son, be wise' (xxvii. 11). What directions for wise living do you find in xxvii. 5-22, especially in regard to friendship?

(3) What, according to xxvii. 23-27, is the reward of diligence? See also xxvii. 18, xxviii. 19; Rom. xii. 11 (R.V.).

Notes.—(1) xxvii. 16. The meaning is uncertain. The LXX has a different rendering: 'The north wind is a harsh wind, but it has an auspicious name' (Moffatt).

(2) xxvii. 21. See R.V. 'By his praise', i.e. by the praise he receives. The judgment of those in the midst of whom a man lives discovers his true worth. Cf. xxxi. 31.

(3) xxvii. 25, 26 should more probably read, 'When the hay is removed and the after-growth appears, and the grass of the mountains is gathered, then thy lambs will supply thee with clothing, and thy goats furnish the price of a field' (I.C.C.).

Day 5. Pr. xxviii and xxix.

(1) Gather out in these chapters the verses which present a contrast between the righteous and the wicked. How do these differ in character and conduct? Consider also their influence for good or evil upon society, especially if they hold positions of authority.

(2) What is said about the importance of keeping the law, and what about a right attitude to the poor? There are four references to the first, and at least five to the second.

(3) Put a mark against verses in these two chapters that you feel to be specially incisive and memorable.

Day 6. Pr. xxx.

The last two chapters of Proverbs are appendices. Chapter xxx gives the words of Agur, of whom nothing further is known. The chapter should be read in the R.V., where the different sections of which it is composed are clearly shown. Agur first looks Godward, and is humbled by the mystery of the divine being and power. Later he looks out upon the world of men and animals and notes a number of striking facts, which he records.

(1) Notice the definiteness, urgency, content and motive of Agur's prayer. Compare with it the prayer which our Lord taught His disciples to pray.

(2) Are the 'generations' or classes of men mentioned in verses 11-14 still present? State in four words the sins of which they were guilty.

(3) What four lessons may the four animals mentioned in verses 24-28 teach us?

Day 7. Pr. xxxi.

(1) What three virtues did King Lemuel's mother urge upon her royal son? Are they any less necessary for all who will occupy positions of responsibility?

(2) Does verse 7 convey that what is wrong as a rule may be right as an exception?

(3) Make a list of the qualities of the ideal housewife as depicted in verses 10-31.

Notes.—(1) Verse 10. 'Virtuous'; the Hebrew word includes both moral worth and practical efficiency. Cf. xii. 4, xiv. 1. Ruth was such an one. See Ru. iii. 11.

(2) Verse 18b. This does not mean that she worked all night, but that her house was well ordered, and ready against emergencies. Cf. xiii. 9.

ROMANS

INTRODUCTION

(See New Bible Handbook, pp. 354-358)

THE Epistle to the Romans was written from Corinth during three months which Paul spent in the province of Achaia, as described in Acts xx. 2, 3 (R.V.). Its purpose is to present to the church in Rome (which he had not founded, but which he hoped soon to visit) a reasoned statement of the gospel which he preached, together with a discussion of the great problem of Jewish unbelief and of the relation of both Jews and Gentiles to Jesus Christ and His salvation. From xv. 23, 24 it would seem that the apostle to the Gentiles felt that he had done everything possible to carry out his task in the east. The time had now come to put into operation his plans for extending his work westwards. In such a task it would no doubt be advantageous to have the prayerful support and practical fellowship of the church in the metropolis. Rome was a strategic centre and the church there would seem to have been as cosmopolitan as the city. A clear statement of the gospel which he would be preaching would be the best means of clearing up any misunderstandings which might arise through Jewish-Gentile tensions or through other causes, and of gaining for Paul the fellowship and co-operation he desired.

At the outset Paul declares that the gospel is the power of God unto salvation to every one that believes, because in it is revealed a righteousness which comes from God, and is obtained and maintained through faith (see i. 16-17, R.V., the key verses of the Epistle). Then the great themes of human guilt—of free grace and the righteousness which comes from God, of justification by faith, the new life in Christ Jesus, the work of the Holy Spirit, the divine sovereignty, and the inclusion of 'the nations' in God's purposes of love—are unrolled one by one, making the Epistle to many the most marvellous book in the Bible.

ANALYSIS

i. 1-17.	Introduction: the theme of the Epistle stated.
i. 18–iii. 20.	The failure of human righteousness.
iii. 21–v.	God's way of salvation expounded, illustrated, and its excellence displayed.
vi–viii.	Justification by faith in relation to holiness.
ix–xi.	The problem of Israel; God has *not* broken His promise, but will gloriously fulfil it.
xii–xv. 13.	Holiness in practical life.
xv. 14–xvi.	Concluding personal messages.

Week 46. ROMANS I–IV. 15

Day 1. Rom. i. 1-17.

(1) What does the apostle say in these verses about himself? See verses 1, 5, and each verse from 9 to 16. With i. 14 cf. 1 Cor. iv. 1, ix. 16, 17.

(2) What does he say about the gospel, its origin, theme, content, and power?

Note.—Verse 17. The phrase 'a righteousness of God', here and in iii. 21, means a righteousness provided for man in Christ, and has to be distinguished from the phrase 'the righteousness of God' or 'His righteousness' in iii. 5 and iii. 25, 26, which means God's character as righteous.

Day 2. Rom. i. 18-32. Human sin and God's wrath.

(1) How does Paul show the sin of man to be (a) deliberate, and (b) inexcusable? How did it begin, and how result in blindness of heart and in moral degeneration?

(2) How does God's wrath manifest itself? Notice the three stages in verses 24, 26 and 28. Cf. Ps. lxxxi. 12; Acts vii. 42. A

picture of God's wrath at work is seen in the book of Judges
(see Second Year, Weeks 19-21). Do you see it at work in the
world of today?

Note.—Verse 18. 'Hold', better as in R.V., 'hold down'.

Day 3. Rom. ii. 1-16. Principles of divine judgment.

(1) What four things are said about God's judgment in verses
2, 6, 11 and 16? Can you find in the passage any other characteristics of it?

(2) What will be the decisive test in the judgment? See verses
7-10. How will this bring under condemnation the self-righteous
person who, while condemning others, himself also sins? See verses
1, 3 and 4.

Notes.—(1) Verses 7 and 10 in no way contradict the truth that salvation
cannot be earned by works. Paul is not dealing at this point with the method
of salvation, but with the nature of the test in the day of judgment. The test
is righteousness (cf. 1 Jn. iii. 7, 10). If a man is not righteous in heart and life,
he will be condemned. Later Paul will show that the only way to become
righteous is through faith in Christ.

(2) Verses 12-15. The meaning is that men will be judged by the light they
have had. If they have been under the law of Moses they will be judged by
that; if not, they will be judged by the standards they possess by nature through
reason and conscience.

Day 4. Rom. ii. 17-29. The sin of the Jews—pride and formalism.

(1) What ten points does Paul enumerate in verses 17-20, upon
which the Jews of his day were inclined to congratulate themselves? But is racial and religious pride, accompanied by moral
shortcomings, confined only to Jews? If 'Christian' were substi-
tuted for 'Jew', and 'the word' for 'the law', how far would the
argument apply to professing Christians today?

(2) The Jews rested upon circumcision as the seal of God's
covenant with them. But what else does Paul here show to be
required without which the outward sign ceases to have value?
Cf. 1 Sa. xvi. 7. How would you frame the argument in relation
to Christian ordinances?

Day 5. Rom. iii. 1-20. Objections answered, and sin and guilt
shown to be universal.

(1) In verses 1-8 the apostle answers questions and objections
which he found that men raised against the gospel. They are
stated in a very condensed form and, if found difficult, may be
passed over. Notice, however, how Paul describes the Old Testa-

ment Scriptures, to what two attributes of God he holds fast, and what kind of conduct he strenuously repudiates.

(2) In verses 10-18 Paul gives the general verdict of Scripture upon man in his fallen condition. What does Scripture say (a) about the general trend of human life (verses 10-12, cf. Is. liii. 6a); (b) about man's speech (verses 13, 14); and (c) about his conduct and inner attitude to God (verses 15-18)? How does this witness confirm the verdict of experience already given in i. 18-32 and ii. 17-29, and lead to the conclusion of iii. 19, 20?

(3) Do you assent to the truth that it is impossible for any child of man, by his own efforts, to escape condemnation at the bar of God's judgment?

Notes.—(1) Verse 20. 'The works of the law'; a phrase which occurs also in verse 28, and denotes conduct such as may be attained by man's own effort in obedience to a divinely-given statute. Cf. Gal. iii. 10-12.

(2) 'Justified' means 'declared, or pronounced, righteous'.

Day 6. Rom. iii. 21-31. The one way of salvation, revealed in the gospel.

(1) The answer to the question how guilty man can be saved is found in the revelation of a righteousness of God; that is, a righteousness provided by God (see Day 1, Note). It will help greatly to clarify what is said about this righteousness in this all-important paragraph of the Epistle (verses 21-26) if the various points are written down one by one. There are fifteen in all.

(2) What two inferences follow? See verses 27, 28 and verses 29, 30, and cf. 1 Cor. i. 29-31; Gal. iii. 28. And what is Paul's answer to an objector who might say that the gospel of salvation by faith, which Paul preached, made the law of no account?

Notes.—(1) The whole of this passage should be read in the r.v., which makes many points clearer.

(2) Verse 27. The term 'law' (*nomos*) is used in this verse in rather a different sense from that which it has elsewhere in this passage. Perhaps the nearest equivalent word in English to the meaning here is 'principle' (see r.s.v.).

Day 7. Rom. iv. 1-15. The witness of Scripture.

Paul has made three statements which were directly opposite to the Jewish interpretation of Scripture. The first was in iii. 20, that by the works of the law shall no flesh be justified; the second in iii. 30, that God would justify Gentiles through faith without circumcision; and the third in iii. 19 and 28, that salvation is given independently of the law. Paul proceeds, therefore, in chapter iv to show that Scripture supports these propositions. He bases his argument mainly on Gn. xv.

(1) Abraham, and David also, were men pre-eminently in the favour of God (see, e.g. Is. xli. 8; Acts xiii. 22). On what basis, then, according to Scripture, was righteousness reckoned to them? See verses 1-8.

(2) At what *time* in Abraham's life was his faith reckoned to him as righteousness? Was it before or after his circumcision? How does this vitally affect the question at issue regarding the admission of Gentiles? See verses 9-12.

(3) The Jews thought that the promise to Abraham and his seed was bound up with the observance of the law. How does Paul show that the very opposite must be true, in the nature of the case? See verses 13-15.

Week 47. ROMANS IV. 16–VIII. 17

Day 1. Rom. iv. 16-25. The correspondence between Abraham's faith and ours.

(1) Consider, for example,

    (a) The promise to Abraham (Gn. xv. 5-7) and the corresponding promise to us (Gal. iv. 5-7).

    (b) The inability of Abraham in himself (verses 18, 19) and our corresponding inability. See iii. 20.

    (c) The God in whom Abraham believed (verse 17) and the God in whom we believe (verse 24).

    (d) The result to Abraham (verse 22) and to us (verses 23, 24a).

(2) In what sense are our sins and our justification the cause of Christ's death and resurrection, as stated in verse 25? Cf. Is. liii. 4-6, 8b, 11; 1 Pet. ii. 24; 1 Cor. xv. 17.

Day 2. Rom. v. 1-11. Is justification by faith real and lasting?

(1) What immediate blessings does it bring? See verses 1 and 2. Can you say 'Amen' to these in your own experience?

(2) Someone, however, may say: 'But what of the tribulations attending the Christian life? Do they not detract from its blessedness?' What is Paul's answer to this? See verses 3-5.

(3) Verses 6-10 expand the latter part of verse 5. What is the proof of God's love? And what assurance does this give respecting the future?

Notes.—(1) The A.V. is to be preferred in verses 1-5, but in verse 11 read the reconciliation' as in R.V.

(2) The whole argument of the passage turns upon the words 'and not only so' in verses 3 and 11. It shows that the Christian has three grounds of confidence regarding his salvation: (a) present experience; (b) God's love meeting us in tribulation; and (c) God Himself (verse 11). The argument of verse 11 is similar to that of viii. 31, 32. Notice the thrice-repeated 'Rejoice' in verses 2, 3, 11 (R.V.).

Day 3. Rom. v. 12-21. The universality of sin and death more than met by the universality of salvation in Christ.

(1) In what respects does Paul show God's salvation in Christ to be far mightier for good than man's fall in Adam was for evil?

(2) What four 'reigns' are spoken of in this passage? Two of them are known to all in sad experience. Are we beginning now to know the other two in glad experience through Jesus Christ our Lord?

Note.—The passage should be read in the R.V.

Day 4. Rom. vi. 1-14.

The Christian has died to sin in Christ's death and lives now to God through union with Christ in His resurrection. Paul here regards sin under another aspect—as a tyrant power holding men in bondage. The only way of escape from sin as a tyrant master is to die to it, and this has been made possible for us in Christ.

(1) For those who are spiritually united with Christ, what is now their position (a) in relation to sin, and (b) in relation to God? And how has this change been effected?

(2) This being our position in Christ Jesus, how are we to abide in it so as to live in daily experience a life of victory over sin? See verses 11-14, noting particularly the expressions 'reckon', 'let not', and 'present' (R.V.).

Notes.—(1) The passage should be read in the R.V. The question in verse 1 arises out of what Paul has said in chapter v. 20b.

(2) Verses 3-10 are an exposition of verse 2.

(3) Verse 6. 'Our old man' means 'the man we were of old', subject to sin. 'The body of sin' means 'the body in which sin ruled', whose members were employed in sin's service (see verses 13 and 19).

(4) Verse 7. A statement of the general principle that death ends all obligation and relationships (cf. vii. 1, 2), here applied to our former relationship to sin. 'Justified from sin' (R.V.) means 'acquitted from any claim sin makes upon us as its slave'.

Day 5. Rom. vi. 15-vii. 6. Not under law, but under grace.

Two questions may arise out of the statement of vi. 14: the first, 'Shall we then continue to sin?' and the second, 'How is it possible to be not under law?' The first is answered in vi. 15-23, and the second in vii. 1-6.

(1) In vi. 15-23 what two masters are contrasted? What kinds of service do they respectively demand, and with what result? In view of all these things, what is the only possible answer to the question whether we should continue in sin?

(2) To answer the second question (How is it possible to be not under law?) Paul finds in the marriage tie an illustration of a person being subject to law and subsequently set free from it (verse 1-3), and applies it to the case of the Christian (verse 4). In the case of the Christian, by whose death is his old position under law brought to an end? Who is the new husband? And what are the fruits of this new union, as contrasted with those of the old (see verses 5, 6)?

Notes.—(1) vi. 23. Read '*In* Christ Jesus our Lord' as in R.V. Cf. 1 Jn. v. 11.

(2) vii. 4. When Christ's body was broken in death, He passed to a life free from all subjection to legal ordinances and we, having died with Him, are also set free. Joined to Him in His resurrection life, life henceforth is to be lived, not in legal bondage, but in the glad obedience of love.

Day 6. Rom. vii. 7-25. Life under the law—its inevitable failure and misery.

(1) Verses 7-13. The phrase 'the sinful passions which were through the law' in vii. 5 (R.V.) might suggest that *the law itself is sinful*. What evidence does Paul give in these verses to show that the law is holy and good, and yet (a) reveals sin; (b) provokes sin; (c) results in death; and (d) thereby brings to light the exceeding sinfulness of sin?

(2) Verses 14-25. Which is the stronger force in a man's life, the law or sin? What, then, is the inevitable result of life 'under the law', even at its best?

Note.—In verses 14-25 the apostle expands what he means by the phrase 'the oldness of the letter' (vii. 6). The law of God commands from without, but sin as a power *within* compels obedience to its own dictates. Two things are needed. (a) deliverance from the condemnation which the law of God pronounces, and (b) a power within greater than that of sin to enable us to do God's will. Both are provided in Christ, as Paul shows in chapter viii, expounding the meaning of his words 'newness of the spirit' (vii. 6).

Day 7. Rom. viii. 1-17. Life in the spirit—its sure victory.

(1) Verses 1-4. What is the happy condition of those who are 'in (union with) Christ Jesus'? Paul explains in verses 3 and 4 (a) how their deliverance has been brought about; (b) what God's purpose is in effecting it; and (c) how those must walk who would experience it.

(2) Verses 5-11. Life according to the flesh, and life according to the Spirit, are here contrasted in tendency and in result (verses 5-8). What is it that effects the change from life in the flesh to life in the Spirit? And how does life in the Spirit carry with it also ultimate victory over death?

(3) Verses 12-17. What, then, is our duty? And what are our privileges?

Notes.—(1) The passage should be read in the R.V.

(2) Verse 2. The Spirit, sin, and death are regarded as powers exercising authority, and the Spirit proves the stronger. Cf. Gal. v. 16, 17.

(3) Verse 3. 'In the death of His own Son, who has come in our nature to make atonement for sin, God has pronounced the doom of sin, and brought its claims and its authority over man to an end' (Denney).

(4) 'Flesh' here denotes our corrupt human nature. To 'walk after the flesh' is to follow its cravings. The flesh is not destroyed in us, but the deeds which it would do can be 'mortified' or made dead (verse 13).

Week 48. ROMANS VIII. 18–XI

Day 1. Rom. viii. 18-39. Present sufferings the prelude to glory.

The apostle comes back to the fact of present suffering and expounds more fully chapter v. 3-5.

(1) What threefold ground of confidence does Paul give in verses 18-27 that the present time of suffering will issue in glory? See verses 18-22, 23-25 and 26-27, noting the three occurrences of the word 'groan' or 'groanings'. Cf. Ex. ii. 23-25.

(2) In verses 28-39 how many distinct reasons does Paul give for the Christian to rejoice, though everything in this world should seem against him?

Day 2. Rom. ix. 1-13. God's word has not failed.

In chapters ix–xi Paul deals with the great problem of the rejection of their Messiah by the bulk of the Jewish nation, and God's consequent rejection of them. Two questions arise: (a) Has God broken His promises? and (b) If not, how are they to be fulfilled? Paul answers the first question in chapters ix, x, and the second in chapter xi.

(1) Chapter viii is full of triumphant joy. How, then, can Paul speak of having great sorrow and unceasing pain in his heart? What made him sorrowful? How much of this Christian joy and how much of this Christian sorrow do we ourselves know?

(2) Verses 6-13. The question with which Paul is here dealing is: If God rejects those Jews who reject Jesus as Messiah, has not His word come to nought? For were not the promises (verse 4) made to the Jews? How does Paul answer this question? And

what two principles of God's election does he find in the Old
Testament stories of the births of Isaac and of Jacob and Esau
respectively?

Day 3. Rom. ix. 14-29. The sovereignty of God.

(1) How does Paul show that in His election of men God retain
absolute liberty of action (a) without compromising His own
righteousness, and (b) without giving man any just ground of
complaint? See verses 14-22. At the same time observe how Paul
lays emphasis upon God's *mercy*. See verses 15, 16, 23-26.

(2) Applying these principles, what Scriptures does Paul cite to
show that what was happening, both in regard to the exclusion
of the bulk of the Jews and also in regard to the admission of the
Gentiles to become the people of God, was nothing new in God's
dealings, and therefore need not be a stumbling-block to faith?

Day 4. Rom. ix. 30–x.
The cause of Israel's failure is shown to be their refusal to accept God's way
of righteousness.

(1) What are the two ways of seeking acceptance with God
which are here contrasted? And how are they shown to be mutually exclusive? See ix. 30–x. 9.

(2) Righteousness by faith (verses 8-15). What does the apostle
say regarding (a) its simplicity; (b) its universal application; and
(c) the necessity of proclaiming it?

(3) What light do verses 16-21 throw upon man's responsibility
in hearing the gospel? Observe also with what skill the apostle
shows that the faith of the Gentiles and the disobedience of Israel
are all foretold in the Scriptures. The word of God, therefore, far
from coming to nought (ix. 6), was actually finding fulfilment
in what was taking place.

Day 5. Rom. xi. 1-10.
The rejection of Israel is in part only, not total.

(1) What three reasons are given in this portion to show that
God has not cast Israel wholly away?

(2) How have the remnant who have been saved come into
that blessedness? And how have the others failed to obtain salvation? What has been God's part in the result, and what man's?

Day 6. Rom. xi. 11-24.
The rejection of Israel is for a time, not final.

(1) If a man trips and stumbles he may either rise again or

fall and perish. What reasons does Paul give here for his confidence that Israel's rejection is not final?

(2) Against what spirit does he warn Gentile believers? What lessons ought we to learn for ourselves from God's dealings with Israel?

(3) How does this passage encourage the vigorous prosecution of missions to the Jews?

Notes.—(1) Verses 11, 12. The noun 'fall' in these verses might be better translated 'lapse'. It is from a different root from the verb translated 'fall'.

(2) Verse 16. See Nu. xv. 17-21. As the offering of the first fruits was regarded as consecrating the whole harvest, so in the choice of the patriarchs the whole nation became set apart for God. Cf. verse 28.

Day 7. Rom. xi. 25-36.

(1) By what Scriptures does Paul confirm that Israel shall yet be saved?

(2) Consider the plan of God as here revealed. By what successive steps has God already acted, and will still act, to bring about the result stated in verse 32? Test your insight into the marvel of God's plan by the measure in which you spontaneously enter into the doxology in verses 33-36.

Notes.—(1) Verse 25 (last clause). Cf. Mk. xiii. 10; Lk. xxi. 24.

(2) Verses 26 and 27. The quotation up to verse 27a is from the LXX of Is. lix. 20, 21; that of verse 27b is from Is. xxvii. 9. Cf. also Zc. xii. 10, xiii. 1.

Week 49.   ROMANS XII–XVI

Day 1. Rom. xii. Practical Christian living—in the Church.

Chapters xii and xiii form a new section of the Epistle, in which the apostle sets forth the practical life of the believer: first, in the religious sphere as a member of the Church (xii); and second, in the secular sphere as a member of the state (xiii). The starting-point is the dedication of our bodies to God, to live, not according to the practices of the world, but to do His will (xii. 1, 2). The goal is the return of the Lord (xiii. 11-14).

(1) Fundamentally, what should be the believer's conscious and deliberate attitude (a) to God, and (b) to the world? What will be the result?

(2) It has been suggested that the teaching of verses 3-8 might be summed up in the word 'humility', and that of verses 9-21 in the word 'love'. How far is this true?

(3) Take one by one the precepts of this chapter, and ask yourself of each—Am I living thus?

Notes.—(1) Verse 1. 'The mercies of God'. The reference is partly to the latter part of chapter xi, but also to the whole promise for deliverance from the guilt and power of sin, as expounded in chapters iii–viii.

'Your reasonable service'. Cf. 2 Cor. v. 14, 15 ('We thus judge' means 'We have come to the considered judgment').

(2) Verse 20. 'Coals of fire'. A figurative emblem of severe pain, here the pain of shame and contrition.

(3) The whole passage should be read in the R.V. and from a Bible with references.

Day 2. Rom. xiii. Practical Christian living—in the world.

(1) What three main reasons does Paul give in verses 1-5 why it is right to submit to the civil power? And how will this submission express itself in practice?

(2) What single guiding principle should control the Christian's life in society? See verses 8-10.

(3) Verses 11-14 (forming the close of the section xii-xiii). Paul gave in xii. 1 one powerful motive to live the life set forth in these chapters, namely, 'the mercies of God'. What further motive does he present here? What will wearing the 'armour of light' mean in practice, negatively and positively? Am I so living?

Day 3. Rom. xiv. Mutual consideration.

There seems to have been in the church in Rome a minority who felt themselves bound in conscience by religious scruples, which those of a more robust faith did not share. The apostle addresses both classes in verses 1-12, and then in verses 13-23 addresses himself specially to 'the strong'.

(1) What rules does Paul lay down in verses 1-12? Can you find four reasons why it is wrong to judge other Christians in such matters?

(2) Verses 13-23. What should 'the strong' be concerned about most in their relation to their weaker brethren? What danger arises if 'the strong' act with a high hand? What are the most important things to be preserved at all costs in a Christian community?

(3) If in doubt ourselves about the lawfulness of a thing, can we do it because we see other keen people doing it? If not, why not?

Notes.—(1) Verse 1. The meaning seems to be that the Church should make the weaker brethren welcome, but avoid argument in their presence.

(2) Verse 5. There is no need to suppose that Paul was thinking of the weekly sabbath here at all, but rather of Jewish holy days.

(3) Verse 6. There is an important principle here, akin to that of verse 23b. It is that if we can *thank God* in what we do, receiving it as His gift, it is right to do it; otherwise not.

Day 4. Rom. xv. 1-13. True brotherhood.

(1) The counsel given in verses 1-2 is by no means easy to

follow. What three sources of help and encouragement are suggested in verses 3-5? And what glad result will follow if success is achieved (verse 6)?

(2) What Scriptures does Paul select to show that it was God's purpose from the beginning to save both Jews and Gentiles in Christ?

(3) Why the emphasis on 'hope' in this passage? See verses 4, 12, 13. Does division among believers tend to increase depression? What, in contrast, ought to be the life of Christians, as expressed in verse 13?

Day 5. Rom. xv. 14-33. Paul's work and plans.

The Epistle from i. 16 onwards has been more like a treatise than a letter. Now Paul resumes the epistolary form, and there are many links between this closing section (xv. 14 to end) and i. 1-15.

(1) How does Paul in verses 15-21 describe his work—in relation to its nature, scope, power, and results? How far is this description applicable to our own work in connection with the gospel?

(2) What matters lay nearest to Paul's heart at this time, as shown in verses 20-29? Also, what may we learn about the importance which he attached to intercessory prayer? Have we a kindred spirit and outlook?

Notes.—(1) Verse 16. The figure here is that of the sacrifices of the Old Testament ritual. Paul's work was to bring Gentiles to God as an offering, sanctified by the Holy Ghost. See R.V. mg.

(2) The contributions of the Gentile churches to the poor of the church in Jerusalem were the result of much labour on Paul's part, and he looked for important results in the closer drawing together of Jewish and Gentile believers. See 2 Cor. viii and ix, especially ix. 12-15.

Day 6. Rom. xvi. 1-16. A glimpse of some early Christians.

(1) What may we learn about Phœbe from her name and the place where she lived (see notes below), from the description of her as 'sister' and 'servant of the church', and from the service which she rendered? What did Paul ask for her from the Christians at Rome, and on what grounds?

(2) Looking down the list of names, note the references to (a) diligent service; (b) sufferings borne for Christ; and (c) Christian character. Cf. 2 Cor. v. 9, 10 (R.V.).

(3) How often do you find the phrase 'in the Lord' or 'in Christ Jesus' or 'in Christ'? Notice also the different connections in which it is used. Have we not here the inner secret of the Christian life, service, and fellowship of the early Church?

Notes.—(1) Verse 1. The name Phœbe, being that of a goddess, suggests that Phœbe had a heathen background. But now she is a 'sister' in the Lord, one of the household of faith (cf. Eph. ii. 19). 'A servant of the church', not necessarily in any official capacity, but a church worker. 'Succourer of many' (cf. xii. 13). Cenchrea, the eastern part of Corinth, was not an easy place in which to live as a Christian.

(2) Verse 7. 'My kinsmen'. This probably means 'fellow countrymen'. 'Fellow-prisoners'. They may at the time have been imprisoned with Paul for the gospel's sake. 'Of note among the apostles'. Outstanding Christians, holding apostolic office.

(3) Verse 10. 'The approved' (R.V.). One whose life had stood the test.

(4) Verse 13. Rufus. Possibly the same as the Rufus of Mk. xv. 21. 'Chosen in the Lord', that is, a choice Christian, one of special quality.

Day 7. Rom. xvi. 17-27.

(1) (a) How may perverters of the gospel be recognized? See 1 Tim. vi. 3; Mt. vii. 15-20. (b) How may we be safeguarded from them? Cf. 2 Jn. 10; 2 Tim. ii. 14-16; 1 Thes. v. 22. (c) What encouragement have we in the conflict?

(2) Verses 25-27. How is God described? How does the present age differ from all that went before? What is the one all-important end to be achieved? Cf. i. 5. What is the method to be adopted?

Note.—The 'mystery' spoken of in verse 25 is fully expounded in the Epistle to the Ephesians. See e.g. Eph. iii. 3-6.

ECCLESIASTES

INTRODUCTION

(See New Bible Handbook, pp. 201-203)

THIS book speaks through the mouth of Solomon, but does not in any way build on his authority. In the earlier part the writer describes human life as seen by a shrewd observer, who controverts the arguments of those who find a satisfactory aim in life either in intellectual labour, or in the gathering of riches, or in pleasure, or even in the attainment of an ethical ideal, seeing that death terminates all, and comes to all alike.

Man cannot by searching find out the deep things of God (iii. 11) but must bow before His sovereignty (iii. 14). Whatever appearances may indicate, God judges righteously, though judgment be long delayed (viii. 12, 13).

The recurring phrase 'under the sun' may be regarded as indicating the purely human standpoint adopted by the writer in the earlier chapters, and as roughly equivalent to 'in the world as

man sees it'. It is most helpful for the Christian to contrast the vanity of this world, its business and pleasures, as set forth in Ecclesiastes, with our glorious heritage in Christ as set forth in the New Testament. For the great glory of the Lord Jesus is that he fills life with meaning, and makes abundantly worth while all that is done along the lines of His will, so that life is the very opposite of 'vanity'.

The book is the inspired record of a spiritual pilgrimage, reaching its culmination in chapter xii (cf. xii. 13, 14 with Rom. ii. 16). In Ecclesiastes, perhaps more than in any other book of the Old Testament, the standpoint of the writer should be borne in mind, and particularly the fact that he saw nothing for man beyond death save judgment. His attention is concentrated upon this life, for 'our Saviour Jesus Christ, who abolished death, and brought life and incorruption to light through the gospel' (2 Tim. i. 10, r.v.), had not yet appeared.

ANALYSIS

i. 1.   The title.

i. 2–11.   The endless monotony of human life on earth.

i. 12–ii. The Preacher's experiences—wisdom, pleasure, labour alike fail to satisfy. 'There is nothing better for a man than to eat and drink and enjoy himself, as he does his work' (ii. 24, Moffatt's translation).

iii–vi.   Further illustration of the vanity of man's striving. His life is hemmed in by divine control, and ends in death. Various counsels. Riches do not satisfy.

vii–xi. 8. The kind of life men should lead. Wisdom is better than folly. The fear of God brings a sure reward. God's works are unsearchable. Various counsels.

xi. 9–xii. Childhood and youth pass; old age and death draw near. The ultimate conclusion; fear God and keep His commandments.

Week 50. ECCLESIASTES

Day 1. Ec. i and ii.

The book opens (i. 2, 3) with a statement of one of its main themes, namely, the futility and unprofitableness of human life and labour 'under the sun'. See *Introduction*.

(1) i. 4-11. How is the unchanging *sameness* of man's experience from age to age brought out in these verses? Contrast the Chris-

tian's outlook as given in such scriptures as Lk. i. 78, 79; 2 Cor. iv. 6, v. 17.

(2) How did the Preacher discover by personal experience that neither the pursuit of wisdom (i. 12-18), nor the enjoyment of pleasure (ii. 1-11), can satisfy man's heart?

(3) Though wisdom is better than folly (ii. 13, 14a), what three facts rob even wisdom of its power to satisfy? See verses 14b-17, 18 and 23, 24-26.

Notes.—(1) i. 2. 'Vanity of vanities'; i.e. vanity in the highest degree; 'utterly vain' (Moffatt).

(2) i. 3. 'Under the sun'; a phrase occurring 29 times in the book.

(3) i. 7, 8. The R.V. is clearer here, as also in i. 11, ii. 3, 8, 21, 26.

(4) i. 14. 'Vexation of spirit'; better, 'a striving after wind', as in R.V.; i.e. something quite futile.

(5) ii. 25. 'More than I'; read as in R.V. mg., 'apart from Him', i.e. from God.

Day 2. Ec. iii–iv. 8.

(1) iii. 1-15. The Preacher here elaborates the truth, already expressed in ii. 24-26, that everything is in the hand of God. What instances does he give to show that the sovereign control of God extends over all human life? Cf. Mt. x. 29, 30.

(2) What in the light of this does the Preacher declare to be the best use of life? See verses 12, 13. The Preacher comes back repeatedly to the same conclusion; see, e.g., ii. 24, iii. 22, v. 18, viii. 15, ix. 7-9. But what other note is sounded in verse 14, which also is heard throughout the book? Cf. v. 7, vii. 18, viii. 13, xii. 13.

(3) In iii. 16–iv. 8 what four instances does the Preacher give of the futility of life, and what reflections did they awaken in his mind?

Notes.—(1) iii. 1. 'Season . . . time'; the two words express two thoughts, (a) that everything happens at an appointed time, and (b) that the time is appropriate in relation to the working out of God's purpose. Cf. Ps. xviii. 30a.

(2) iii. 11. Read as in R.V. The meaning of this difficult verse seems to be that while God has placed in man's heart desires that go beyond the temporal, yet man cannot grasp His plan. This also is a thought repeated in later chapters. See vi. 12, viii. 16, 17.

(3) iii. 16. Wickedness and iniquity in the seat of law and government.

(4) iv. 4-6. 'Also I saw that human toil and skill mean jealousy between man and man. . . . He is a fool who folds his hands, and lets life go to ruin. Still, one handful of content is better than two hands full of toil and futile effort' (Moffatt).

(5) iv. 7, 8. The picture of a miser.

Day 3. Ec. iv. 9–vi.

(1) What are the advantages of companionship, as described in
iv. 9-12? How does this apply in the spiritual life? See, e.g., Mt.
xviii. 19; Mk. vi. 7; Lk. x. 1; Acts xiii. 2, xv. 12.

(2) What does the passage v. 1-7 teach concerning worship, in
respect to (a) the right attitude of spirit, (b) words spoken in God's
presence, (c) the importance of carrying out promises made?

(3) What does the Preacher say in v. 8–vi concerning riches
and rich people?

Notes.—(1) The R.V. is clearer n many verses. See especially iv. 12, 14-16,
v. 14.

(2) iv. 13-16. The picture of a youth rising by wisdom to be king, though
born poor and in prison. At first all the people were with him, hailing him as
ruler (verses 15, 16a); yet the next generation did not favour him (verse 16b).
The persons alluded to in these verses are quite unknown.

(3) v. 1. 'Keep thy foot'; that is, 'never enter God's house carelessly'
(Moffatt).

(4) v. 3. As cares and labours cause a man to dream, so do many words in
worship give rise to folly.

(5) v. 8, 9. The meaning here is obscure.

(6) v. 20. 'Then he will never brood over the fewness of his days' (Moffatt).

(7) vi. 10, 11. 'Whatever happens has been determined long ago, and what
man is has been ordained of old; he cannot argue with One mightier than
himself' (Moffatt). In verse 11 read as in R.V. mg. The meaning is that much
talking against God's dealings is profitless.

Day 4. Ec. vii and viii.

The Preacher has declared several times that man's best course in this
present world is to enjoy the portion in life which God has given him, and the
fruit of his labour. See Day 2 (2). In these later chapters, while still holding
to this view, he enquires more closely into the kind and quality of life which men
should lead.

(1) What does he commend, and what discountenance in vii.
1-10?

(2) Gather out the varied counsels given in vii. 11–viii. 5. See
notes below, and with vii. 16 compare Lk. xiv. 25-27.

(3) In spite of life's anomalies (viii. 10, 14) and the insoluble
riddle of it all (viii. 17), of what one thing is the writer sure concerning the final end of the righteous and the wicked?

Notes.—(1) The R.V. should be read in vii. 7, 11-12, 21, viii. 1, 10.

(2) vii. 14. 'Anything that shall be after him'; i.e. what is to happen. Cf.
vi. 12.

(3) vii. 18. 'Shall come forth of them all'. Moffatt translates: 'shall avoid
both extremes'.

Day 5. Ec. ix–x. 7.

(1) What two facts govern man's life on earth (see ix. 1 and ix. 2-6)? In view of these facts the Preacher can reach no other conclusion than what he has said before. See ix. 7-10 and Day 2 (2). In what does it fall short of New Testament standards?

(2) What illustration is used in ix. 13–x. 3 to show the value of wisdom? Yet how little is it honoured (ix. 16), and how easily marred (ix. 18b–x. 1)!

(3) What two faults to which rulers are prone are mentioned in x. 4-7?

Notes.—(1) The R.V. is clearer in ix. 1, 7, 12, 17, x. 1, 4.
(2) x. 2. 'A wise man's sense will keep him right; a fool's mind leads him wrong' (Moffatt).

Day 6. Ec. x. 8–xi. 8.

(1) Today's portion gives counsel on various matters. Make a list of these. The main thought is that men should be diligent in work in spite of possible danger or loss.

(2) x. 8-15. How is it shown in these verses (a) that no useful work can be done without the possibility of unexpected danger (see Note 1 below); and (b) that wisdom is needed?

(3) When human life and activity is thus beset by many limitations and uncertainties, ought we to do nothing? What is the Preacher's answer in xi. 1-8? Cf. Day 2, Note (4).

Notes.—(1) x. 8-10. The word 'shall' in these verses is better rendered 'may'.
(2) x. 11, 19. Read as in R.V. The last clause of verse 19 seems to mean that where there is money, there is full supply.
(3) xi. 1, 2. 'Trust your goods far and wide at sea, till you get good returns after a while. Take shares in several ventures; you never know what will go wrong in this world' (Moffatt).
(4) xi. 8. 'The days of darkness'; i.e. which follow death. Cf. ix. 5, 10.

Day 7. Ec. xi. 9–xii.

(1) In the Preacher's counsel to youth (a) in what is youth to rejoice? (b) to what all-important fact are they to give heed? and (c) whom are they to remember? What further summons does the New Testament give? See Mk. i. 15; 2 Tim. ii. 1. With xii. 1a cf. Pss. ciii. 2, cxix. 55.

(2) Contrast with the picture of old age and death the joyful

hope to which we are begotten by the resurrection of our Lord.
Cf. 2 Cor. iv. 16-18; 2 Tim. iv. 6-8; 1 Pet. i. 3-5.

(3) In summing up man's duty, what place does the Preacher
give to God? How was this perfectly exemplified in Jesus (cf. Jn.
xiv. 31), and in Him made possible for us all? See Mt. v. 48;
Rom. viii. 3, 4; Heb. xiii. 20, 21.

Notes.—(1) xi. 10. 'Vanity' has here the meaning of 'transitory' or 'passing'.
(2) xii. 2. Old age compared to winter weather, when storm succeeds
storm.
(3) xii. 3-6. A series of pictures of the failure of man's various bodily faculties
in old age, such as strength of limb, number of teeth, keenness of sight, etc.
'When old age fears a height, and even a walk has its terrors, when his hair
is almond white, and he drags his limbs along, as the spirit flags and fades'
(Moffatt's translation of verse 5).
(4) xii. 11. See R.V. Both A.V. and R.V. renderings probably refer to inspired
scriptures, which, whether they are goads to prick the conscience, or strong
nails or pegs (typifying trustworthiness), are alike from the one Shepherd.

GALATIANS

INTRODUCTION

(See New Bible Handbook, pp. 364-368)

THE particular situation with which the Epistle deals must be
kept in mind if its great argument is to be understood. Paul had
preached the gospel of salvation by faith in Jesus Christ to the
Galatians, who were of Gentile race. They had welcomed him
with enthusiasm, and many had believed (iv. 14, 15). But they
had later been visited by Jewish-minded Christian teachers who
had told them that it was not enough simply to believe on Jesus
Christ: they must also be circumcised, and keep the Law of Moses.
These teachers had further cast doubts upon Paul's apostleship,
and had sought to undermine his authority. We can understand
with what mingled sorrow, indignation and deep concern Paul
refutes the teaching of the legalists, and defends both his own
position and the truth of the gospel, which he had proclaimed.

The question at issue assumes a different form today, but is
none the less vital. Is acceptance with God to be obtained by any
effort of ours, or is it, as the gospel declares, the free gift of God's

grace through the redemptive work of Christ, to be obtained by
faith alone? The enduring value of this Epistle lies in the answer
given by Paul, under the inspiration of the Spirit, to this question.

ANALYSIS

i. 1–10. Introduction.
i. 11–ii. 21. Paul declares that the gospel which he preached
is not of human origin, but came to him by the
revelation of Christ.
iii. 1–v. 1. Acceptance with God is not obtained by doing
what the law commands, but by faith in Jesus
Christ.

iii. 1–9. The facts of their own experience con-
firmed by the case of Abraham.
iii. 10–14. The hopeless position of those under
the law, from which the death of
Christ alone delivers.
iii. 15–18. The original covenant of promise is not
superseded by the law.
iii. 19–24. The true function of the law.
iii. 25–iv. 7. The blessedness of those who have believed in Christ.
iv. 8–20. Appeal not to backslide.
iv. 21–v. 1. The spiritual freedom of the believer
illustrated from 'the law' itself.

v. 2–vi. 10. The life of the Christian: (a) faith, hope, love;
(b) walking in the Spirit.
vi. 11–18. Conclusion.

Week 51. GALATIANS

Day 1. Gal. i.

(1) What does Paul say in verses 1-10 (a) about God, (b) about
Christ, (c) about himself, (d) about the gospel? Note these things
carefully, for they lay the foundation on which the Epistle rests.

(2) What four statements about the gospel are made in verses
11 and 12? Paul demonstrates the truth of these statements in the
rest of chapters i and ii, by giving a review of his life-story.

(3) What five periods in his life are described in verses 13-24?
Are there any points where his experience touches yours?

Note.—Verse 10 is parenthetical. Paul appears to have been charged by his opponents with being a man-pleaser, and interjects after writing verses 8-9, 'Am I now seeking the favour of men or of God?' (r.s.v.) that is, 'words such as I have just written do not look like man-pleasing, do they?'

Day 2. Gal. ii.

(1) What two further incidents in his life does Paul refer to in this chapter and how do they help to demonstrate the truth of i. 11-12?

(2) Observe Paul's courage. What does he say twice over was his chief motive in taking so firm a stand? See verses 5 and 14. What may we learn from this?

(3) Consider in verses 16 and 20 how clearly Paul states, first, the sole ground of acceptance with God, and second, the inward principle of the Christian's life. Can you give the assent of your experience to each clause of these two verses?

Notes.—(1) Verses 1-10. In this visit of Paul and Barnabas to Jerusalem, Paul in a private talk with the leaders of the church laid before them the gospel which he was preaching among the Gentiles (verse 2), with the result that they acknowledged his call to the apostleship of the Gentiles, and gave him the right hand of fellowship (verses 6-10). An effort was made during the visit, by some in the church, to insist on Titus, a Gentile believer who was with Paul, being circumcised, but Paul did not yield (verses 3-5).

(2) Verses 15-18. Jews generally regarded uncircumcised Gentiles as 'sinners' and unclean, and there were some even within the church who thought that by eating with uncircumcised Gentiles, they made themselves 'sinners' (cf. Acts x. 28). Paul's contention was that the real transgressor was the man who having accepted justification by faith, sought to rebuild the barrier of the Law (verse 18).

Day 3. Gal. iii. 1-18.

These verses are a fourfold argument in proof of ii. 16. (a) Verses 1-5, an argument from experience, (b) verses 6-9, an argument from Scripture teaching about Abraham, (c) verses 10-14, an argument from the meaning of Christ's death, and (d) verses 15-18, an argument from the fact that the covenant of promise was long prior to the giving of the law.

(1) Try to state the substance of these arguments in your own words.

(2) Consider the phrases 'by the works of the law' and 'they that are of the works of the law' on the one hand, and 'by the hearing of faith' and 'they that be of faith' on the other. Show how they express radically different principles.

(3) How does Paul show that faith in Christ has from the very beginning been God's plan, and the only way of salvation?

Notes.—(1) Verses 1-5. Paul in his visit to Galatia had set clearly before his hearers Christ crucified, and they, through believing, had received the Spirit (cf. Acts xiii. 52), and suffered persecution in consequence. 'By the hearing of faith' (verses 2 and 5) is an abbreviated expression for hearing the Word of the gospel, and receiving it with faith. Cf. Rom. x. 8-17.

(2) Verse 7. 'The children of Abraham'; in the sense of spiritual likeness. Cf. Jn. viii. 39.

(3) Verses 8, 9. Paul interprets the promise of Gn. xii. 3b to mean that just as Abraham received the blessing of justification by faith (Gn. xv. 6), so a time would come when men of all nations would 'in Abraham', i.e. through his seed, which is Christ (verses 14, 16), receive the same blessing in the same way.

(4) Verse 15. 'I speak after the manner of men'; i.e. I take an illustration from human life. Some translate 'covenant' here, by 'will', but it makes no difference to Paul's point. Even a human covenant or will, if once ratified, stands, and cannot be altered. How much more then must God's covenant stand firm! Cf. Heb. vi. 13-18.

(5) Verse 16. It is not by chance, Paul says, that Scripture speaks of 'Abraham and his seed'. For God all through had looked forward to Christ as the one in whom His promise was to be fulfilled. Cf. 2 Cor. i. 20.

Day 4. Gal. iii. 19–iv. 7.

(1) iii. 19-24. See *Analysis*. Paul has seemed to make light of the law, and his opponents might ask, 'Wherefore then serveth the law?' Can you find in these verses five purposes which the law serves?

(2) iii. 25-29. What are the privileges of believers as here set forth? Write them down in your own words.

(3) What, according to iv. 5, is the purpose of our redemption, and what amazing privilege is said in iv. 6 to flow from our filial relationship to God in Christ?

Notes.—(1) iii. 19, 20. 'Added because of transgressions'; i.e. the law gave to sin the form of transgression and so made men conscious of guilt before God when they sinned. Cf. Rom. iii. 19, 20, v. 20, vii. 7, 13.

'It was ordained by angels by the hand of a Mediator' ('intermediary,' R.S.V.). Paul introduces these words to show that the promise is superior to the Law even in the very manner of its promulgation. In the case of Abraham God Himself spoke the promises directly, whereas the giving of the law was through intermediaries on both sides—God being represented by angels (cf. Dt. xxxiii. 2 (LXX); Acts vii. 53; Heb. ii. 2), and the people by Moses.

(2) iii. 24. 'Schoolmaster'; better, 'custodian', as in R.S.V. The Greek word denotes a guardian attendant, appointed to watch over the sons of a household when young.

(3) iii. 26. Read 'sons' as in R.V., not 'children'.

(4) iii. 27. 'Put on' here means 'take the standing or position of', i.e. to have the standing of Christ before God.

(5) iv. 3. 'The elements of the world'; R.V., 'rudiments'; R.S.V., 'elemental spirits'. The meaning is uncertain. It seems best to take it as meaning rudimentary teachings that do not rise above this world, and are merely types and

shadows of heavenly realities (cf. Heb. viii. 5, ix. 1, x. 1). Paul calls them in verse 9 'weak and beggarly', i.e. without power, and without resources, unable to deliver men from the world (cf. i. 4) and give them the position of sons and heirs of God.

Day 5. Gal. iv. 8–v. 1.

(1) iv. 8-20. Paul pleads with the Galatians not to backslide. What plea does he use in verses 8-11, and what in verses 12-20?

(2) What indications are there in these verses that Paul regarded the situation with the utmost gravity and with great distress of heart? Are we beginning to know something of a concern for souls such as Paul had? See 2 Cor. xi. 28, 29; 1 Thes. iii. 6-8.

(3) iv. 20–v. 1. Paul suddenly decides to present the teaching he has been giving in the form of a *picture*, taken from Gn. xvi, from a part of the Scriptures which the Jews specially called 'the law'. In this picture, what is the position of those who are 'under the law', and what in contrast is the portion of believers? Cf. Eph. ii. 18, 19.

Notes.—(1) iv. 12. The meaning seems to be: 'I, a Jew, have become as you, a sinner trusting alone in Christ for salvation. Do you, then, become as I am', i.e. hold fast to the same position. The last clause of the verse is best taken with what follows, and should be translated, 'In nothing did you wrong me'.

(2) iv. 17, 18. 'They zealously seek you in no good way' (R.V.). A reference to the new teachers, who were eager to win the favour of the Galatian believers in order to cut them off from Paul and his gospel so that they would have no one to turn to but themselves. If these teachers had really come to do good, Paul would have raised no objection (verse 18).

(3) iv. 20. 'I stand in doubt of you'; better, 'I am perplexed about you', as in R.V.

(4) iv. 26. 'Jerusalem, which is above'; cf. Heb. xii. 22.

(5) iv. 27, 30. Paul quotes two Scriptures to show that the future lies with believers, and not with the party of the law.

Day 6. Gal. v. 2-24.

Spiritual freedom may be lost in two ways, (a) by false teaching, in this case the teaching of the necessity of circumcision (verses 2-12), and (b) by living to please self (verses 13-15). The secret of victory is to give the Holy Spirit full sway within us; He will subdue the flesh, and bring forth in us the fruit of holiness (verses 16-25).

(1) To be circumcised meant taking the way of the law. What four results would follow if they did so? What in contrast is the way of the gospel (verses 5-6)?

(2) Verses 13-15. How should the Christian use his freedom? Cf. Jn. xiii. 12-17; Lk. xxii. 26.

(3) Verses 16-24. The Christian has within him 'the flesh', i.e. his fallen sinful nature, and the Spirit, and he must take sides in the conflict between them. What must be his attitude to the flesh (verses 16, 24) and what to the Spirit (verses 16, 18); and how will this be manifested in his life and character (verses 22-24)? Observe the simplicity of the gospel way of holiness. Are you proving it in experience?

Notes.—(1) Verse 5. 'The hope of righteousness'; i.e. the hope of future glory that springs from justification through believing on Jesus Christ. Cf. Rom. v. 1, 2; 1 Pet. i. 3. Notice in verses 5-6 the collocation of faith, hope and love, as in 1 Cor. xiii. 13; 1 Thes. i. 3.

(2) Verses 16, 17. Life for the Christian is not, as it were, an open way, in which he can walk where and as he pleases. It is a battlefield. But if he 'walk in the Spirit', i.e. let the Spirit rule and regulate his inner life, there will be victory over the flesh.

(3) Verse 18. The Christian is free from the law as a rule of life, yet, led by the Spirit, he does that which the law approves (verses 22, 23).

(4) Verse 24. The self-life, condemned, is nailed to Christ's cross. Cf. ii. 20; Rom. vi. 6.

Day 7. Gal. v. 25–vi.

(1) In v. 16-24 the apostle has spoken of the life of the Christian in his individual character; in v. 25–vi. 10 he speaks of the Christian's life in his social relationships. What will the result of walking in the Spirit be in that sphere? Make a list of what you find, and test your own relation to fellow-Christians by it.

(2) vi. 11-18. If we would be Christians after the pattern of Paul, what will be our attitude to the cross? Gather up what is said about the cross in this Epistle. What reasons can you discover why Paul esteemed the cross so highly?

Notes.—(1) vi. 2. 'The law of Christ'; cf. Jn. xiii. 34; 1 Jn. iv. 21.

(2) vi. 3-5. It is not good to compare oneself with another, and to glory over him. For that is to glory only in respect of another's shortcomings. In the judgment each will have to bear his own burden—the things he himself has done. Cf. 2 Cor. v. 10.

(3) vi. 8. 'Soweth to the flesh'; acts of self pleasing:
'Soweth to the Spirit'; acts of obedience to the Spirit.

(4) vi. 11. 'How large a letter'; better, 'with how large letters', as in R.V. Usually, it would seem Paul wrote the closing salutation in his own writing (1 Cor. xvi. 21; 2 Thes. iii. 17), but in this case he wrote more, possibly the whole letter.

(5) vi. 12, 13. Paul's opponents gloried in new additions of circumcised believers, because this gave them favour in the eyes of fellow-Jews.

THE SONG OF SOLOMON

INTRODUCTION

(See New Bible Handbook, pp. 203-206)

THE Song of Solomon is beloved of Christians not so much because of its exquisite literary charm, its rich appreciation of the beauty of nature and its deep insight into the human heart, as because they find in it a parable of heavenly realities. It speaks to them of the love of Christ for His Church, and gives to them words in which to utter their hearts' devotion to Him.

It is uncertain who wrote it. The phrase 'which is Solomon's' in i. 1 may equally mean 'which is for Solomon' (as in the title of Ps. lxxii) or 'which is about Solomon'; and there is no other clue to its authorship.

According to the earlier and more usual interpretation, there are only two main characters—Solomon and his bride. Many commentaries of great devotional beauty and insight have made this interpretation familiar, in which the bride is regarded as a type of the Church, and Solomon of Christ. An analysis of the Song, based upon this view of it, will be found in the *New Bible Handbook*.

Others, however, discern in the background of the story another figure, the figure of a shepherd, who is the bride's true lover. It is he whom she called 'my beloved'. A maid from the village of Shulem, she had gone one day to visit her garden, when she fell in unexpectedly with some of Solomon's retinue, who took her captive to the palace (vi. 11-13). There the king visits her, and struck by her great beauty seeks to win her for himself. But she has a shepherd lover to whom her heart is pledged, and to whom she remains faithful. Three times the king visits her, wooing her with growing ardour, until at last, finding all his efforts of no avail, he sets her free. At the close of the book she is seen leaning on the arm of her beloved, returning to her village home, where she is received by her family and friends as the shepherd lover's acknowledged bride.

An analysis of the book, based on this interpretation, is given below. It will be seen that, in this view, much of the book consists of reveries in which the bride communes in thought with her beloved, and of incidents and dreams connected with him, which with artless simplicity she tells to the ladies of the court. In this view of the book the shepherd lover is a type of Christ, and Solomon a type of the world, against whose enticements the soul remains faithful to Him to whom its love is pledged.

We must form our own views on these questions from the study of the book. But whichever interpretation be adopted, the book remains a spiritual picture of the mutual love of Christ and His people, and a precious treasure to His own.

ANALYSIS

SECTION I. i. 2–ii. 7. *Scene in the private apartments of Solomon's palace.*

    i. 2–8. The maid, soliloquizing, expresses her longing for her absent lover (2-4). Then, seeing the ladies of the court eyeing her, she explains to them the darkness of her complexion (5, 6), and breaks out into a cry that she might know exactly where her lover is (7), to which the ladies of the court reply that she should go to seek him (8).

    i. 9–11. The king enters, praises her beauty, and promises to adorn her with jewels.

    i. 12–ii. 6. The king having gone to his repast, the maid falls into a reverie, in which, in imagination, she communes with her beloved in some forest glade.

    ii. 7. She bids the ladies of the court not to seek to arouse love by artificial means.

SECTION II. ii. 8–iii. 5. *The bride relates an incident of the past.*

    ii. 8–14. Her beloved came one morning to call her to go with him.

    ii. 15. She is sent instead by her brothers into the vineyard. Cf. i. 6.

    ii. 16, 17. She bids her beloved return at the end of the day.

    iii. 1–4. When he did not return, she could not rest, but went out into the night to seek him.

    iii. 5. The same charge as in ii. 7.

SECTION III.   iii. 6–viii. 4. *The struggle is intensified, but ends in victory.*

iii. 6–iv. 7.   Solomon, appearing in royal splendour, makes a determined attempt to capture the maid's affections.

iv. 8–v. 1.   Alarmed, she flees in thought to her beloved, whose voice she hears, bidding her escape with him from the dangers of the palace (8). He pours out his love for her in words far excelling the conventional tributes paid to her by the king (9-16a). Her heart opens to him, and she sees their marriage day as if already come (16b–v. 1).

v. 2–16.   The bride relates a disturbing dream which she has had; and in answer to a question from the ladies of the court gives an impassioned description of her beloved.

vi. 1–3.   The ladies of the court ask where he is, that they, too, may seek him, a suggestion that leads the bride to declare that no other can share her privilege of possession.

vi. 4–10.   The king enters, and tells her in words of admiring praise that there is none who can compare with her, and that even his queens have sung her praises.

vi. 11–13.   The bride interrupts to explain how she came to be in the king's palace.

vii. 1–9.   The king continues to urge his desire.

vii. 10–viii. 3. The bride, refusing, turns in heart to her beloved.

viii. 4.   The same charge as in ii. 7 and iii. 5.

SECTION IV.   viii. 5–14. *The scene is the bride's village home.*

viii. 5.   The bride, released, returns with her beloved to her home.

viii. 6, 7.   The bride's panegyric on true love.

viii. 8–12.   She recalls her brothers' words, and declares her faithfulness.

viii. 13, 14. Her lover bids her speak and in the presence of his friends she calls him her beloved.

Week 52. SONG OF SOLOMON.

N.B.—The questions below are based upon the Revised Version.

Day 1. Ct. i. 2–ii. 7. See *Analysis*.

(1) i. 2-8. 'Thy love is better than wine', 'Draw me, we will run after thee', 'We will be glad and rejoice in thee', 'O thou whom my soul loveth'. Does our heart speak thus of Christ?

(2) ii. 3, 4. Consider the two figures by which the bride expresses the bliss of communion. See notes 5 and 6 below. Have we experienced that Christ gives comfort, rest and refreshment, and that he leads us into a place of delight, protected by love? Cf. Ps. lxiii. 3-5.

Notes.—(1) i. 5, 6. The bride's brothers in the heat of anger sent her to the vineyards.

(2) i. 12-14. Women wore small bags of myrrh, suspended from the neck under their dress. To the bride, her beloved was as the costliest perfume.

(3) i. 15, the shepherd speaks; i. 16–ii. 1, the bride; ii. 2, the shepherd; ii. 3-7, the bride.

(4) ii. 1. The bride describes herself as an ordinary wild flower of the meadow (see R.V. mg.).

(5) ii. 3. 'Apple-tree'; giving shade (3b-4) and fruit (3b).

(6) ii. 4. 'Banqueting house'; literally 'house of wine' (R.V. mg.), signifying 'a place of delight'.

(7) ii. 7. A difficult verse, which seems to mean that love should awake or come to life of itself, and not by artificial stimulation.

Day 2. Ct. ii. 8–iii. 5.

(1) How does this portion illustrate the trial of being prevented from enjoying some anticipated opportunity of communion with Christ by the opposition of others? See *Analysis*, and compare the position of the Psalmist in Pss. xlii and xliii.

(2) iii. 1-4. What characteristics of true love are seen in these verses? Cf. Ps. cxix. 2, 10; Je. xxix. 13; Lk. xv. 4 ('until he find'). Notice, too, the name by which four times she describes her lover. Is this our own attitude to Christ?

Note.—ii. 17. A picture of evening, not (as A.V.) of early morning. The shadows flee away, when the sun that causes them sets. The bride hoped for a meeting with her beloved in the cool of the evening, when he returned from the 'mountains of separation' (R.V. mg.), but was disappointed. Night came, and her heart still sought him (iii. 1).

Day 3. Ct. iii. 6–v. 1.

(1) iii. 6–iv. 7. See *Analysis*. A picture of the glory and allurement of the world. Cf. Ec. ii. 4-8; Phil. iii. 8; Gal. vi. 14; 1 Jn.

ii. 15, 16. Are you like the bride of the song, faithful to the Lover of your soul, or like Demas? See 2 Tim. iv. 10, and in contrast, Phil. i. 20, 21.

(2) iv. 8-15. Is it possible that Christ should find such delight in His people? Yet see Pss. cxlvii. 11, cxlix. 4; Is. lxii. 5b; Jn. xv. 9, 10; Eph. i. 18 (last clause), v. 25-27.

(3) iv. 16b. Are we willing to open the garden of our inner life to Christ, to do there what He will? Is our heart reserved for Him alone (iv. 12)? Cf. Is. xxvi. 13.

Notes.—(1) iii. 6. 'Pillars of smoke'; fragrant columns of smoke arising from burning incense.

(2) iii. 7. 'Litter'; in verse 9 'Palanquin', a couch covered by a canopy borne by four or more men.

(3) iv. 4. The neck, decked with ornaments, is compared to a battlemented tower, hung with shields.

(4) iv. 8. The bride hears the voice of her beloved, calling her to himself. The verse seems to be a poetic description of the dangers to which she is exposed in the palace.

Day 4. Ct. v. 2–vi. 3.

(1) v. 2-8. This dream (see note 1 below) may teach important lessons. Why did the bride not respond to her beloved (verse 3)? and what did she suffer in consequence? How may we apply these things to ourselves? Cf. Ho. v. 15; Rev. iii. 20.

(2) What is the answer in our hearts to the question of v. 9? Do we rejoice to tell of Christ? Is He to us the chiefest among ten thousands and 'the altogether lovely One'? Cf. the doxology in Rev. i. 5, 6 and the description of Rev. i. 12-16.

Notes.—(1) v. 2. The words 'I was asleep' indicate that the bride is relating a dream.

(2) v. 4. The door was bolted, see verse 5.

(3) v. 10. 'The chiefest among ten thousand'; literally, 'marked out by a banner' (see R.V. mg.); i.e. distinguished from all others as a standard bearer is distinguished, and hence 'pre-eminent'.

Day 5. Ct. vi. 4–viii. 4. See *Analysis.*

(1) The glowing intensity and purity of the bride's love for her beloved gave her a look that inspired a sense of awe in the beholder. Ought not the qualities mentioned in vi. 4 and 10 to be also found in Christ's Church? Cf. Acts ii. 43a, iv. 13, 33, v. 11.

(2) Compare together the three similar utterances of the bride in ii. 16, vi. 3 and vii. 10. Would you say that in Christian experience the order is as follows: (a) Christ's love, 'His desire is towards

me' (vii. 10; cf. 1 Jn. iv. 19); (b) our acceptance of Him, 'my beloved is mine' (ii. 16, vi. 3); (c) the yielding of ourselves to be His, 'I am my beloved's' (ii. 16, vi. 3, vii. 10)? Have we made this surrender?

(3) vii. 13. What fruit are we laying up for our Lord? Cf. Rom. xv. 16-17; Phil. ii. 16.

Notes.—(1) vi. 4. 'Tirzah'; the name (meaning 'delight') of a beautiful town, which later became the royal residence of the kings of northern Israel. 'Comely as Jerusalem'; cf. Ps. xlviii. 2.

(2) vi. 9. 'Choice'; or 'pure' (R.V. mg.); in verse 10 translated 'clear'.

(3) vi. 12, 13. A possible translation is 'My soul has unwittingly brought me to the chariots of the companions of my prince'; i.e. she fell in with some of Solomon's retinue. She fled, but they called her back, and gazed upon her, as she put it, as if she were a company of dancers.

(4) vii. 1-6. These verses may be part of the song composed by the women (vi. 9b and 10), or may be spoken by Solomon. In verses 7-9 he is certainly the speaker.

(5) vii. 11–viii. 3. The bride's refuge from Solomon's advances is always to commune in spirit with her beloved. Cf. i. 12–ii. 6, iv. 8 ff.

(6) viii. 4. Cf. ii. 7, iii. 5.

Day 6. Ct. viii. 5-14.

(1) 'Leaning upon her beloved'. Are you learning this secret of blessedness in relation to Christ? Cf. Jn. xv. 4, 5; Phil. iv. 13.

(2) viii. 6, 7. If this be true of human love, how much more must it be so of the love of God! Cf. Rom. viii. 35-39. Is our love to Christ of this pattern?

(3) viii. 10. The bride of the story was as a wall in her constancy. Are we thus loyal to Christ, willing to let the world and all it offers go its way if we may but possess Him? Cf. Phil. iii. 8; Rev. iii. 4, 5.

Notes.—(1) viii. 5. 'Under the apple-tree I awakened thee'; that is, the apple-tree overshadowing the bride's home had been their trysting-place; as also the place of the bride's birth.

(2) viii. 6. 'Set me as a seal', etc.; in ancient times men carried their seal fastened to breast or wrist for safe preservation. The bride would ain be thus held fast on the heai ıand arm of her beloved.

'Jealousy is cruel as the grave'; better, 'ardent love is unyielding as Sheol'.

(3) viii. 8-10. The bride's brothers had waited to see if she would be as a wall against temptation, or as an open door to give it entrance. Now she claims that she has shown herself as a wall.

(4) viii. 11, 12. Solomon appears to have offered her a vineyard of great wealth; but she put it aside in favour of the vineyard which was hers in her beloved.

(5) viii. 13. The beloved speaks. 'Thou that dwellest in the gardens'; cf. i. 6, viii. 11. 'Companions'; cf. i. 7.

Day 7. Revision.

How did the bride of the story remain faithful under such great temptation as met her in Solomon's palace? It has been said that it was by the exercise of four things:

(a) Memory—thinking constantly of her beloved.
(b) Fear—the fear of losing him.
(c) The practice of his presence.
(d) Hope—the hope of being reunited with him.

Does your study of the book confirm this, and if so, what application has it to ourselves in relation to our Lord?